THE THAMES IRON WORKS

1837 - 1912

Laurence Ince

Lightmoor Press

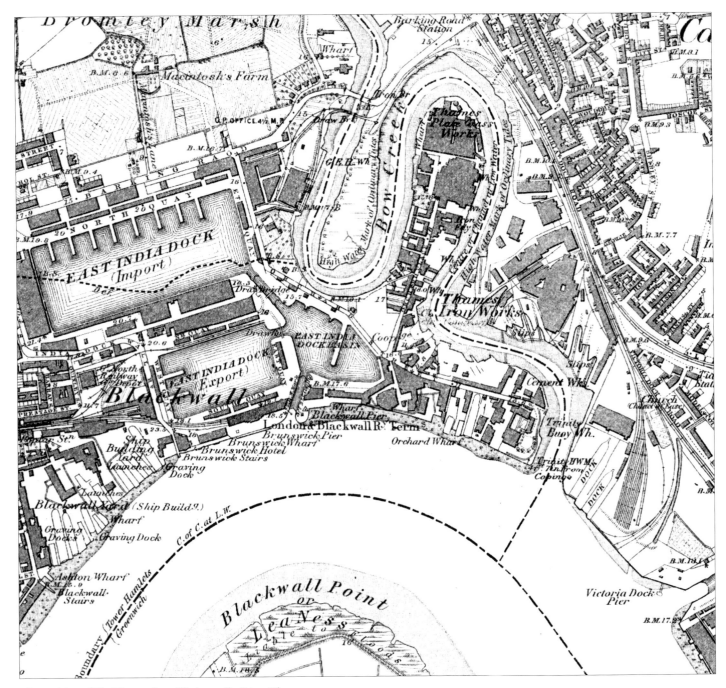

The position of The Thames Iron Works on the River Thames

CONTENTS

LIGHTMOOR PRESS

© Lightmoor Press, 2021
Designed by Michael Day
British Library Cataloguing-in-Publication Data. A catalogue record for this book is available from the British Library

ISBN 13: 9781911038900

LIGHTMOOR PRESS
Unit 144B, Lydney Trading Estate, Harbour Road, Lydney, Gloucestershire GL15 4EJ
www.lightmoor.co.uk
Lightmoor Press is an imprint of Black Dwarf Lightmoor Publications Ltd

Printed in Poland – www.lfbookservices.co.uk

H.M.S. "Thunderer."

Launched by

Mrs. Randall Davidson on 1st February, 1911.

The attractive colour print commemorating the launch of HMS Thunderer. *This was given away as an insert in the 1911 edition of the* Thames Iron Works Gazette.

INTRODUCTION

My early interest in industrial history was aided by the purchase of the important book *The Stationary Steam Engine* by George Watkins. This was first published in 1968 although my purchase of the volume can be dated to the early 1970s. Each engine received a large photograph and a page of text explaining its construction and how it was used in its industrial setting. Engine photograph 42 was a set of four triple expansion pumping engines at work at the Walton Waterworks of the London Metropolitan Water Board. These engines were completed in 1911 by the Thames Iron Works. The reference to an ironworks on the Thames intrigued me and started my interest in this company. I knew of large scale ironworks situated on the coalfields of South Wales, the English Midlands, Lancashire, the North East and Scotland. Each of the works situated in these areas made iron by using furnaces but did that happen on the Thames? Of course not, the Thames Iron Works did not make their own iron for it was an engineering works that used iron to produce ships, structural iron and many other engineering products. The title of the concern was for many years the Thames Iron Works Company. It always used the two words iron and works in their advertising, share certificates and official company documents. The joined up ironworks only made an appearance on company material during the period 1911 to 1912 on the cover of their own magazine. This was in the last years of the life of the company when much was hoped for with the launch and completion of HMS *Thunderer*. To commemorate this event a copy of the works' magazine was resurrected for publication in 1911. It was a rather rushed out copy of the old works' magazine with a new format and it was at this juncture that the mistake was made. The concern should always be known as Thames Iron Works.

Much has been written about the Thames Iron Works but little about its historic engineering history. References to the works often describes the importance of the company in fostering sport. The Thames Iron Works Football Club is quite rightly praised as being the forerunner and inspiration for the West Ham United Football Club. Football at the Thames Iron Works was part of the paternalistic development of the ideals of Arnold Hills of how a modern industrial concern should treat its workers. Under his management he wanted to provide his workers and families with sporting teams, clubs and societies that would allow them to use their spare time in a productive manner. He tried to alter how workers were paid at Thames and founded a works magazine, *The Thames Iron Works Gazette*. The gazette that he published would educate, inform and also record the progress of the company. At the end of the nineteenth century the works was organised in a manner that would be more apparent in an industrial concern seventy five years later. Truly Arnold Hills was ahead of his time with regards to the organisation of this great industrial concern that he loved. It has been a rare privilege to follow in his footsteps while exploring the history of the Thames Iron Works.

I must thank the staff of the London Metropolitan Archives for their help and advice when examining the records of the Thames Iron Works which they have in their care. One important part of this account is the list of ships that the Thames Iron Works built. However, this list posed many problems with the consistent recording of the names of the vessels. This problem was mainly related to the ships built at the yard for foreign customers. In the documentation produced by the works you often find names of these ships spelt in two or even three different ways. To solve this problem I have tried to discover what the ships were known by in the countries that purchased them and so I have used these versions of their names. I am grateful to Malcolm Bobbitt for writing the chapter on the motor vehicles built by the Thames Iron Works. He has certainly added greatly to the story of the progress of the Thames Iron Works and increased my knowledge of the company's activities. I would like to thank Ian Pope and Neil Parkhouse of Black Dwarf Lightmoor Publications LTD for their support in bringing my researches to publication. The vast majority of the illustrations in this volume are from my own collection. The photographic record of the Thames Iron Works was brought about by the dedication of the Hills family in producing a magazine that recorded in detail the progress of the company. It was a far-sighted decision which allows us now to follow the life of the Thames Iron Works in detail.

LAURENCE INCE, Solihull, 2021

Chapter 1

MARINE ENGINEERING AND THE RIVER THAMES

At the beginning of the nineteenth century the area around the River Thames was the most important shipbuilding centre in Great Britain. A large number of ships were built on the Thames and this manufacturing work was recognised as being of the highest quality. London, being a great trading city, generated a high demand for new ships. Capital was readily available and so was skilled labour. The presence of the offices of the Admiralty in the city also guaranteed a demand for locally built ships. London was the centre of government, the site of the royal court and the largest market of consumers in England. The city was also home to a large number of merchant houses who acted as agents for farms, plantations and commercial firms dotted around the British Empire. Often machinery and ships were ordered through these London based merchants.

The early part of the nineteenth century was a period of great technological change. In the late eighteenth century the invention by James Watt of the separate condenser had revolutionised the design of steam engines. In 1800 Watt's patent came to an end which initiated a great interest in the development of new designs of steam engines. Soon smaller compact engines were being produced. Richard Trevithick was an advocate of high pressure steam engines and his compact design allowed him to produce dredging engines that could be mounted on boats. His engines could also be adapted to be used as railway locomotives. In 1801 William Symington was commissioned by Lord Dundas to engine a steamboat, the *Charlotte Dundas*, for experiments on the Forth. The *Charlotte Dundas* in March 1802 towed two loaded vessels each of 70 tons burthen for a distance of 19½ miles in six hours against a strong adverse wind. These experiments led to the development of Henry Bell's *Comet* which was used for regular traffic in 1812 on the Clyde. In 1805 Boulton & Watt's Soho Foundry had early experience of marine engineering when it built a steam engine to power a boat designed by Robert Fulton. This paddle steam engine was used on a boat on the River Hudson. By 1820 no less than 41 steamboats had been built on the Clyde. After a slow start Boulton & Watt's Soho Foundry had built no less than 77 sets of marine steam engines by 1830. The importance of the London engineering market is shown by Boulton & Watt's activities in the city. This Midlands' firm kept a branch office in London and also had workshops and tools stored on the ship *Pallas*, a Thames-side hulk.[1]

One drawback to the use of steam engines on boats had been the worry of fire with wooden hulls. However, in the early nineteenth century more use was being made of iron in many different structures. Advances in the manufacture of iron had improved the quality of the product and had brought about a decrease in price. As early as 1787 John Wilkinson had successfully launched an iron barge onto a Midlands' canal. John Wilkinson wrote to a friend, '*Yesterday week my iron boat was launched: It answers all my expectations and had convinced the unbelievers who were 999 in every thousand*'. The boat was built at Willey in Shropshire and was thus built only three years after the great improvement in rolling iron plates. Sir Samuel Bentham had built some copper boats and had shown one in 1794 on the Thames. A passenger iron barge, *Vulcan* was launched in 1819 for use on the Forth and Clyde Canal. This boat apparently remained in existence until 1865. However, the first important demonstration of an iron-hulled vessel powered by a steam engine took place in 1821. In that year the ship *Aaron Manby* steamed from London to Paris. The vessel was an iron hulled boat made in sections by the Horseley Ironworks in Tipton. It was powered by an 80hp engine. Soon other firms were constructing iron ships. The father of the famous iron shipbuilder, John Grantham, was responsible for another early iron steam vessel. It was also built by the Horseley Ironworks between 1823 and 1825 and sailed to Ireland for service on the River Shannon. Thirty years later this boat was still afloat and working. During the 1820s iron ships were built by John Grantham of Liverpool, David Napier and William Neilson of Glasgow and John Laird of Birkenhead. Laird continued to build iron ships and in 1833 launched an iron paddle steamer named *Lady Lansdowne*. It was a 148 ton paddle steamer made for the City of Dublin Steam Packet Company. This vessel was transported in parts and put together again in Ireland.

During the 1830s the techniques and skills of iron shipbuilding began to spread across Britain. By this time London already was home to several builders of steam engines. These firms included John Penn & Son and Maudslay, Sons & Field. Both firms had built marine steam engines for the Admiralty and had earned high reputations for their skills and quality of work. In 1831 the East India Company invited tenders for four iron steamboats and four other vessels. Maudslays bid for the contract and won the order. On 28th August 1832 the ship, *Lord William Bentinck* was launched at Lambeth. This small vessel became the first iron ship built on the Thames. The four ships were tugs and measured 125ft x 22ft, each powered by two 60hp oscillating engines. The boats only had a draught of 22½ins. When completed each ship was tested on the Thames. They were then disassembled and sent out in sections to India on board another larger ship. The first two, *Lord William Bentinck* and *Thames* were packed into crates and sent out to India on the East Indiaman, *Larkins*. The tugs *Megna* and *Jumna* followed later and by 1836 all the tugs were in service pulling 'flats' up and down the River Hooghly. [2] Even with this interest in iron ships, development was slow and as late as 1842 one expert could comment that:

'Many, therefore, still view the subject (iron shipbuilding) with distrust and regard it as one of the visionary schemes of this wonder working age which will soon be relinquished and forgotten'. [3]

In fact, Maudslay, Sons & Field showed little further interest in iron shipbuilding. The firm preferred to concentrate its resources on the production of steam engines and machinery. However, several other entrepreneurs could see the potential of developing iron shipbuilding on the Thames. One partnership was that of Thomas Ditchburn and Charles J. Mare who were to start a concern that would grow into the Thames Iron Works.

CHAPTER TWO
DITCHBURN & MARE

One of the pioneering concerns that built iron ships on the Thames was the partnership of Ditchburn & Mare. These very differing personalities began shipbuilding at Dudman's Dock, Deptford in 1837. Thomas Ditchburn (1801-70) was an experienced naval architect. He was the marine designer for the firm while Charles Mare seems to have been in charge of the day-to-day running of the business. However Mare's financial acumen seems not to have been of a high standard. Certainly this is illustrated by his later business career and bankruptcies.

Thomas J. Ditchburn was born and educated at Chatham and entered the Royal Dockyard there as an apprentice. At Chatham he was much employed by Sir Robert Seppings in constructing models and making experiments in connection with the many designs and inventions produced by that celebrated naval architect. After the end of his apprenticeship Ditchburn rose to become the superintendent of the large shipbuilding yard of Fletcher & Fearnall at Limehouse, London. At this time steam boats were coming to the fore but the vessels to which steam engines were applied were ill adapted for this purpose. The ships were short and full-bowed. Under his management the yard produced a series of fast paddle steamers for use on the Thames. His experiments at Fletcher & Fearnall's Yard led to the abandonment of the old 'cod's head' form of bow, Ditchburn having introduced a long fine entrance and greater length of vessel generally. He was appointed to this managerial position at the early age of twenty-one and worked there from 1822 until 1837. He believed that Fletcher & Fearnall intended to make only wooden vessels and became convinced that iron was the material of the future. Ditchburn had seen the possibilities of iron as a material for shipbuilding while working under Seppings at Chatham. Seppings devised a system of diagonal strengthening straps or riders which he first tried out in 1811 and which were generally adopted in 1831. These straps were made of thick iron and were securely fixed to the inside of a ship's hull, producing a far more rigid structure. The lack of interest in the use of iron prompted him to leave Limehouse and become a partner in shipbuilding with Charles Mare. [4] This new partnership entered into the manufacture of iron ships in a very serious way.

Mare was born in Staffordshire in 1815 and his father was lord of the manor of Hatherton. His father wanted Charles to follow a legal career and to this end he was placed with a firm of solicitors in Doctors' Commons. On the death of his father Charles Mare left the legal profession and used his inheritance to become a shipbuilder in partnership with Thomas Ditchburn.

The personalities of these partners could not have been different. Ditchburn was seldom seen to smile but was of a wonderfully even temper. Mare on the contrary, was a man of life and spirit, to whom all who came into contact with him became much attached. Consequently he made friends everywhere, but did not always retain them, as being naturally impulsive would frequently give offence on slight occasion and lose them. [5] However, the partnership started off well with the building of the 365 ton ship, *Inkerman*. This was built for the Russian Government and was a successfully fast boat built to pursue pirates in the shallow waters around the Crimea and in the Black Sea. This promising start encouraged others to place orders with Ditchburn & Mare.

Soon a series of Thames paddle steamers were ordered from the firm. However, in 1838 fire destroyed their works completely, including the finest mould-loft on the Thames. Some observers

*Thomas Ditchburn
(1801-1870)*

felt that this disaster could have been the result of the bitter competition between the new iron building firm and the established wooden shipbuilders. It must be stated that fires at the Thames shipyards were common often fuelled by the raw materials of wood, rope and pitch. In fact the firm would suffer another serious fire a few years later. The disaster prompted a move to the Orchard House Shipyard, Blackwall. Shipbuilding had taken place on the Orchard House Estate at an early date with yards previously owned by Gladstone Snook and William and Benjamin Wallis who had gone bankrupt. The area was difficult to reach by road but a new railway had been built and this opened up the area to development. The locality was still very rural with one worker commenting that in the 1840s he noticed the fruit trees in the orchard being in full blossom. He also described the fresh and inviting open country across the creek.

The Orchard House Estate had been a moated house and orchard dating from the sixteenth century. Over the years the building had degenerated into a 'drinking house'. The Wallis yard had built ships there including warships for the Royal Navy during the Napoleonic Wars. In 1824 when William Wallis died he left a shipbuilders' yard, with slips and excellent ways, a blacksmiths' shop, mould lofts, large covered saw-pits, warehouses, sheds, counting house and dwelling house. Across Bow Creek (River Lea) was an underdeveloped marshy area that offered expansion possibilities for the future.

Soon Ditchburn & Mare were building at their new works a series of iron steamers for use on the Thames. One of these ships was *Propeller* which had a novel drive system. Her engines were of 30nhp and her paddles were of single iron blades which dipped vertically and moved back. Publicity for their efforts was gained in 1841 when the firm offered to build Lord Alfred Paget an iron racing yacht of 25 tons called *Mystery*. Ditchburn and Mare claimed that this boat in a race would beat any wooden yacht of a similar tonnage. *Mystery* was a great success and won her owner eleven prizes within two years. [6] The exploits of Paget and his iron yacht attracted many orders to the yard. Progress at the Orchard House shipyard was halted by another disastrous fire in 1840. This fire destroyed three quarters of an engine house which was made of wood, joiners' workshops and two other buildings. The damage to the yard was soon repaired and shipbuilding resumed.

Although Ditchburn & Mare were becoming famous for their iron ships they were also completing the occasional wooden vessel. Ditchburn also designed and built composite ships where iron frames were planked with wood. Many engineers claim the invention of the composite method. Ditchburn did take out a patent in 1841 stating that, *'My invention relates to certain modes of ship and boat building by planking with wood, on frames composed of iron bars, the most convenient form are angle M iron bars'.*

During the period 1845-46 compared with 1838-44 the tonnage produced by the Orchard House Yard increased by about a factor of seven. It had been thought that the firm produced about 100 ships in their ten year existence but it is far more likely that well over 150 ships were produced by the yard, the vast majority being constructed out of iron. It is obvious from these figures that this pioneering shipyard was the most important builder of iron ships in Britain during the 1840s.

The development of the steam ship was closely linked with the designs of Thomas Ditchburn. In 1822 when he started building steam vessels, their average speed did not exceed 8 miles per hour. In a few years he had raised it to 14 miles per hour in wooden vessels. In 1844 he obtained with an iron vessel a speed of 8 miles per hour in dead water at the measured mile. The Admiralty was now ordering steam powered iron ships from various manufacturers. The firm of Ditchburn & Mare was one of the earliest suppliers of these vessels. The first government order for the yard was the Post

Office packet ship *Princess Alice*. Also the first iron ship purchased by the navy was built by Ditchburn & Mare. This was HMS *Recruit* which was an iron sailing brig of 470 tons. Orders soon followed for a series of paddle steamer warships. Such were the advances in marine engineering it was soon realised that HMS *Recruit* was fast becoming old fashioned. It was later taken in by the yard in 1850 and lengthened and converted to a screw steamer. It emerged from the yard as *Harbinger* built for the General Screw Steam Shipping Company.

In 1841 the yard exported a paddle steamer to Australia. This was *Emu* which was built in sections and rebuilt at Sydney in Australia. Such was the demand for iron ships that the shipyard was extended again and again. At one time the demand for space was so great to lay down keels that a small river steamer was built inside a large sea-going one. The stern frame of the large ship was left open so that the small ship could be launched through the opening. It was as though the large ship was giving birth to the smaller vessel. It was stated about these developments at the Orchard House Shipyard that, *'This prosperity was not to be wondered at, for Mr Ditchburn had, by the introduction of iron vessels and scientific forms, literally revolutionised steam navigation'.*

*Charles J. Mare
(1815-1898)*

A fascinating document survives which outlines the charges made for building iron vessel by Ditchburn & Mare in 1843. It lists the following:

The Hull ranges from £16 to £20 per ton builders' measurement, stores, masting, rigging, copper etc and everything else except provisions £3 to £5 per ton
Steam engines, a pair, the collective power of 100 horses   - £48 per hp
150   "   - £47 per hp
200hp, 300hp, 350hp & 400hp - £46 per hp
450   "   - £47 per hp
500   "   - £48 per hp
220, 320 & 420hp - £45 per hp as Maudslay & Co. having patterns etc complete for these powers can furnish at £45. [7]

Ditchburn & Mare's fame led to an important order when they were asked to build a boat for conveying Queen Victoria from Whitehall to Woolwich. For this the firm suggested building a screw steamer. There was much criticism regarding using this new form of propulsion for a royal ship. The vessel named *Fairy* was built in 1845 and was a great success. She was built as a tender for the *Victoria and Albert* but she was also used to ferry guests to Osborne House on the Isle of Wight. *Fairy* was also used by the Admiralty for propeller experiments and for these she was fitted with a variable-pitch screw. The ship measured 145ft x 21ft and was of 317 tons. Her oscillating 42ins x 3ft engines by John Penn & Son drove her at between 12 to 14 knots. The engine speed was 48rpm and was geared up to the incredible propeller speed of 240rpm.This was the first screw vessel in the navy and often achieved a speed of 13 knots. Queen Victoria liked the boat very much and although a tender became in effect a royal yacht. The fame of the products of the Orchard House Yard was soon spreading. This encouraged the ordering of some large steamers for the Peninsular & Oriental Company.

Another interesting paddle steamer was the *Anglia* which was built for the Chester & Holyhead Railway. Later this vessel was sold to the Confederates and used as a blockade runner during the American Civil War.

However, in September 1847 in the middle of this successful period the partnership of Ditchburn and Mare was dissolved. It has already been noted that the characters of these men were completely opposite and the rupture seems to have been accompanied with much acrimony as detailed in *The Times* of 8th May 1848.

Mr Mare, of the firm of Ditchburn and Mare, ship-builders, appeared on a police warrant, charged by his partner, Mr Ditchburn, with using threatening language towards him. There was another warrant taken out by the complainant against a man named Gully, in Mr Mare's employ, for an assault against him but this was not proceeded with, and Gully was now called as a witness for the prosecution.

It appeared that Messrs. Ditchburn and Mare had dissolved partnership in September last, and it was alleged by Mr Ditchburn that his former partner had used threats against him, and instigated Gully to throw him off a ladder with intent to do him some serious injury. Under these circumstances Mr Ditchburn declared that he considered himself in danger of life. The alleged attempt to throw the complainant from the ladder was made while going on board a steam yacht which was building for the Emperor of Russia.

It was stated that the defendant, Mr Mare had promised Gully a sovereign for the attack upon the complainant, and that he said he would have given him £10 if he had broken his neck. This allegation was positively denied by the defendant, and Gully, although he confessed having moved the ladder, by which Mr Ditchburn fell down, asserted that it was done only in pursuance of orders he had received to prevent anyone from going on board the steamer, and the sovereign he had afterwards resolved was due to him in wages and not intended as blood money.

Mr. Ballantine was of the opinion that there was no evidence to implicate Mr. Mare in the alleged attempt to injure Mr. Ditchburn, but he advised the complainant to indict Gully. He recommended Mr. Mare not to molest the complainant or give him any further cause of fear. Mr. Mare gave a promise to that effect.

The warrant was then dismissed. [8]

Perhaps this was the result of commercial strains within the firm. Shipbuilding on the Thames was a precarious affair at the best of times with a long catalogue of bankruptcies being recorded for the industry in the nineteenth century. The tightness of contracts can by gauged from the building of the *Prince Metternich* by Ditchburn & Mare in 1847. This was a 600 ton iron paddle steamer for use on the Danube and Black Sea which was built with a series of penalties implicit in the contract. The ship was supplied to the Imperial and Royal Steam Navigation Company and was described as:

The said vessel to be 178 feet between the perpendiculars and 24ft 6ins beam or thereabouts, the lines or forms to be left to the builder. It shall be fit for river and sea service as far as practical, the same being intended for the navigation of the River Danube and the mouth thereof and the coasts of the Black Sea adjacent thereto, the said vessel shall be well and substantially built, agreeably to the specifications hereunto attached. That the said vessel shall be fitted with a pair of the most improved oscillating marine engines of the collective nominal power of two hundred horse power, the fitness, and goodness and performance of which are hereby guaranteed by the said Thomas Joseph Ditchburn.

That the said vessel with her engines, boilers filled with water, and in every other respect completed for sea going and having on board 120 tons of dead weight, shall not exceed or draw any part more than 6 feet of water, English measure, from the underside of the bottom of the vessel at the lowest part with the above named weights on board, draw more than 6 feet of water, then the following deductions shall be made from the price to be paid by the said builder, &c., that is to say- For one inch one hundred pounds, for two inches, two hundred pounds, for three inches, four hundred pounds, for four inches, eight hundred pounds, for five inches, one thousand six hundred pounds, for six inches, three thousand two hundred pounds and should the vessel draw at any part more than six feet six inches, the purchasers shall have the right to return the said vessels with her engines to the said builder.

That the speed of the said vessel when completely fitted and finished, as heretofore mentioned and referred to, and ready for immediate service, shall not be less than an average speed of fifteen British miles per hour, as the said miles are measured in the River Thames. And the said builders, &c., further agree that, if the speed of the said vessel shall fall short or be less than fifteen miles per hour, as above stipulated, the following reductions shall be made from the price to be paid for the said vessel, that is to say- For one quarter of a mile, the sum of seven hundred and fifty pounds, for half a mile, one thousand two hundred and fifty pounds for three-quarters of a mile, two thousand two hundred and fifty pounds, for one mile, three thousand pounds. [9]

This ship, in fact, exceeded the stipulated speed by three quarters of a mile per hour during squally weather. It was thought that on a fine day and a clear course the ship could reach sixteen miles per hour. The *Prince Metternich* was also two and a half inches under the required draught of water. The cabins of the ship were tastefully fitted with fifty two beds for first class passengers and sixty beds for second class passengers. It was thought that the production of this ship had materially advanced the high shipbuilding reputation of the port of London.

After the dissolution of the Mare & Ditchburn partnership both partners continued in the shipbuilding industry. In 1848 Ditchburn designed and built, *Volna* an iron schooner yacht for the Grand Duke Constantine of Russia. This was probably built at the yard of Robinson & Russell on the Thames. A list of ships designed by Ditchburn includes two which were also built by this same yard and it seems that for a short time he was involved as a naval architect with this firm.

Citizen A, *a Thames paddle steamer built in 1846. This was one of a series of Thames steamers built by the partnership, each was powered by oscillating steam engines manufactured by John Penn & Son.*

CHAPTER THREE
CHARLES J. MARE – SHIPBUILDER

In the late 1840s the Orchard House Shipyard rapidly developed under the sole ownership of Charles Mare (1815-1898). After the departure of Thomas Ditchburn a decision was made to appoint James Ash as the marine architect at the yard. Mare soon purchased marshy land on the Essex side of Bow Creek and began to develop this area for shipbuilding. The two parts of the yard were joined by a ferry or floating bridge that could carry 200 workers at a time. At first the slipways remained on the Blackwall side while the new workshops were built on the opposite bank. Land was recovered at great expense with the use of piles driven down 20 feet to the gravel. Soon two slips were constructed that could accommodate the building of four small steamers. The mills, shipyards and machine shops were equipped with the most modern machinery including steam hammers. This allowed the business to begin to hammer and roll scrap iron into plates and bars for shipbuilding.

The progress of the Orchard House Shipyard was startling as bigger naval and commercial ships were completed in fairly large numbers. At one time Mare launched no less than five ships over a two-week period. The yard's iron production and fabricating facilities increased greatly and soon the works was also competing for civil engineering contracts. These included the construction and building of bridges and dock gates. At this time many of the commercial steamers produced at the yard were really only sailing ships with auxiliary steam engines. In 1853 Mare's yard launched the *Himalaya* for the Peninsular and Oriental Company which was the largest merchant ship of its time. Iron ships were gaining more acceptance and the Orchard House Shipyard was at the forefront of the development of iron vessels. As well as repeat orders from the Peninsular & Oriental Company, Mare was able to secure important orders from the General Screw Steam Shipping Company and the General Steam Navigation Company. Mare's yard also completed seven sections of Robert Stephenson's Britannia Bridge over the Menai Straits. The main tubes each weighed 1,500 tons and Charles Mare went to the Menai Straits in March 1850 when he and Robert Stephenson drove in the last rivet on the bridge. Other structural ironwork was completed including the iron roof of Fenchurch Street Station.

As the works continued to expand, improved medical services were provided for the workers. The cost of this development was covered by a contribution of 1d a week paid by the men earning over 30s a week. The men on lower wages paid half the contribution paid by the higher earners. Mare also helped found the Poplar Hospital after one of his workmen died from blood loss after a works accident. At that time the nearest hospital was in the Mile-End Road. With the industrial development of the area Mare realised that a local hospital was a necessity. [10]

In 1854 it was noted that the yard had careful forms of accounting for tools, materials and various forms of hardware taken from the stores and used in the building of their ships. Perhaps this was a desperate attempt to cut costs as the firm was now making losses on its contracts. It has been stated that the *Pera*, an iron screw passenger ship built for the Peninsular & Oriental Company was launched early in 1855. It was thought that this was carried out to stop her being seized by Mare's creditors. During this period it had become usual for wages not to be paid out until late Saturday night. Often Kennedy, the cashier, when he arrived with the money, had to pass through a turbulent crowd which often put him in fear of his life. [11] An added problem at this time was the construction of six wooden gunboats for the Royal Navy. These were urgently required for use in the Crimean War. It could be that by this time the yard had little experience in building wooden ships. Each gunboat earned the yard £10,000 but were costing the firm much more than that to build. It is believed that it was the construction of these gunboats that finally broke the firm. The yard's naval architect at this time was G.C. Mackrow and he was adamant that it was the building of the gunboats that brought the firm down. Mare was declared bankrupt in September 1855 with unsecured debts of £160,000 and liabilities of £400,000. The accounts of the firm had not been kept well and it took several months to untangle the financial problems left by Mare's management. Two of the works' managers, namely Joseph Westwood and Robert Baillie, looked after the business for a while on behalf of the creditors. Strangely during this period Mare went to Northfleet to manage the business of W. & H. Pitcher when that firm went bankrupt in 1857. [12] Mare's examination in the Court of Bankruptcy took place on 20th May 1856. The difficulty in examining the financial affairs of the yard was partly because of the record keeping of James Campbell. He was paid £1,000 a year to manage the civil engineering department. Campbell had failed to maintain account books and could not monitor the performance of this important department. This had also led to large losses on the contracts for the Westminster and Saltash Bridges.

Charles J. Mare was perhaps not the ideal character to run a great and complicated business such as a shipyard. He was known to be a 'warm supporter of horse racing' and for a long time kept a string of horses at a racing stable in Newmarket. He and his family did not live frugally. His wife moved in court circles, he was a friend of Disraeli and was a familiar figure at Brighton during the season. His lack of financial acumen could be clearly seen in his own domestic spending. He had lost money on his landed estates and Mare's liabilities included a loss of £3,300 on his stud of horses and £38,000 on his shares in the General Screw Steam Shipping Company. On top of this he had spent £16,000 on contesting an election at Plymouth and on running the *Plymouth Mail* newspaper. Although Mare was elected as MP for Plymouth on 7th July 1852 the result was declared void by petition in the following year. One interesting comment was made about Mare in September 1857 when it was stated in *The Times*, that '*After the bankruptcy of Messrs Mare & Co, the extensive ship builders at Blackwall, a great number of the marine store dealers shops in the neighbourhood were closed. The property stolen from the works was estimated at some thousands of pounds per annum'*. It seems that Mare had brilliant ideas regarding building iron ships but little management or business acumen. Mare's shipyard was taken over by Peter Rolt, his father-in-law who was a member of the committee of creditors.

It seems incredible that Mare could almost immediately bounce back and found another large shipbuilding yard. This was the Millwall Ironworks & Shipbuilding Company. In 1859 Mare took over 22 acres of land that had previously been occupied by Scott Russell before his bankruptcy. At first he operated the business under the style of C.J. Mare & Co. It operated successfully for several years before it went bankrupt during the financial crash of 1866. In 1861 Mare was living at Mills Terrace, Hove with his wife Mary who was the daughter of Peter Rolt. Also at this address were his sons Charles and John and three servants.

After the bankruptcy of the Millwall Ironworks Mare seems to have been involved in the London Engineering Company. He was certainly with this firm in 1866 but then drops out of sight. In 1881 his wife and son Charles were listed on the census as living at 7 Osbourne Villas, Brighton. In the next census of 1891 Mare is listed as a lodger at Clapham Road, Lambeth in the home of George and Ellen Beck. His death in 1898 appears to have been little noticed in the journals and newspapers. However, a monument was later built to commemorate his life and placed at West Ham Municipal College. This was made of Sicilian marble and consisted of a bust on a column. At the upper part of the dado was a half model of HMS *Vulcan* and the cap was of marble and had a roll of a bar mill, a double-throw shaft, a spur wheel and an old wood stock Admiralty anchor. It was a fitting reminder of the career of this pioneer iron shipbuilder.

CHAPTER FOUR

PETER ROLT AND THE FOUNDING OF THE THAMES IRON WORKS

The bankruptcy of Charles Mare led to his shipbuilding yard being taken over by a committee of creditors. From this committee Peter Rolt stepped in to take control in 1856. He knew Mare's business history well for he was Mare's father-in law and was an experienced businessman. Rolt was the son of John David Rolt and his wife Sophia Butt. He was born in 1798 in Deptford where both of his grandfathers held senior positions in the town's Royal Dockyard. Rolt entered business as a timber merchant and contractor. He was a director of the Commercial Dock Company and was well connected with regard to shipping and shipbuilding. Rolt was married in 1820 to Mary Brocklebank whose father founded the General Steam Navigation Company. The marriage allowed him to expand his business interests as he formed a shipping company, Brocklebank & Rolt, in partnership with his father-in-law. As well as his shipping connections he was the Conservative MP for Greenwich and Deputy-Lieutenant of Middlesex.

Rolt's first efforts were aimed at completing any of the outstanding shipbuilding contracts. The gunboats that the yard was building for the Admiralty needed immediate attention. They were well advanced and not to quickly finish these vessels at a time of war would be disastrous for the reputation of the yard. The Admiralty agreed to pay £9,700 of the agreed price in advance to complete the vessels. This then allowed the yard to complete the order. [13] This prompted a further naval order of 20 iron mortar vessels of 100 tons at £2,200 each. Six had to be completed in January, six in February and the rest in March. The works was soon busy building a cross-channel steamer for the South-Western Railway Company and another order had come in for a steamer to be delivered to Genoa. The production of the iron members for the Westminster Bridge kept the forge, foundry and rolling mills busy and total wages at the works were reaching £3,500 each week. Some of the departments at the yard were running shifts both night and day and on one tide in April 1856 no less than five vessels were launched. They were three mortar boats, the *Genova* of 2,000 tons and the *Havre,* a 600 ton paddle steamer built for the South Western Railway. After completing the remaining Mare orders it was time to look to the future and so Rolt reformed the company. It was to be called the Thames Iron Works and Shipbuilding Co. Ltd. with an initial capital of £100,000 in the form of £5,000 shares. [14] This meant that Rolt had decided to find investment from fellow engineers and associates and not to bring in wider investment from the public at large. Rolt held five shares and the Maudslay family of the Thames steam engine builders held three shares. Six of the original shareholders were London engineers. D.F. Dykes who was one of the founders of the Thames engine building firm of Humphrys, Tennant & Dykes Ltd. became one of the first directors. [15] Soon the new company were completing their first orders which included *Prince Frederick William* a steamer that was to ply between Dover and Calais. Soon a whole range of ships were being completed by the Thames Iron Works which included two large passenger ships for the Peninsular & Oriental Company. These were *Nepaul* (1859) and *Delta* (1859). C.J. Mare had built at least three ships for this company and it is a mark of confidence in the new company that additional orders were placed at the Thames Iron Works.

The works was also involved in the building of other structures with iron. In October 1858 the

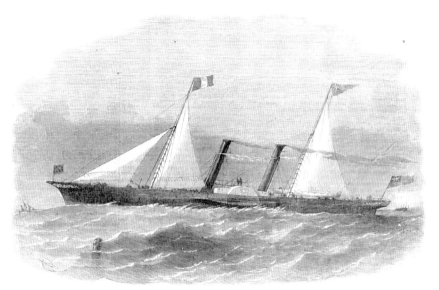

The cross channel steamer
Prince Frederick William
*launched by the Thames
Iron Works in 1857*

Thames Iron Works completed a large floating derrick. This was a large craft made of iron, weighing 5,000 tons which was to be used for raising vessels that had sunk around the British coast. Also at this time a large ship was being built for the Royal Mail Steam Packet Company. This was the *Parramatta* which was to be one of the last ships built at the Orchard Shipyard. Soon a decision was made to concentrate shipbuilding on the Essex side of Bow Creek and reduce production at the Orchard House site. However, the Thames Iron Works continued to hold their property on the Orchard House side of the river.

Much fame was attracted to the company when they were awarded the contract to build HMS *Warrior* in 1859. This was to be Britain's first armoured ironclad battleship. This ship and her sister ship, *Black Prince* were built to match the recent building by the French of the armoured, *La Gloire*. It was thought that the contract was awarded to Thames because of the high quality of their armoured iron. The building of the ship began on 25 May 1859 with the contract for the ship's engines being awarded to John Penn & Son of Greenwich. The *Warrior* was to be, at that time, the largest warship in the world and in the nineteenth century only the *Great Eastern* had a larger iron hull. The ship was praised as being the, *'biggest advance on previous warship designs made in the history of naval warfare'*. It was envisaged that *Warrior* would be launched eleven months after construction started and would be completely finished three months after that. However, with many changes in design asked for by the Admiralty during construction, the project fell behind timetable. In spite of all these problems, *Warrior* was completed more quickly than *Black Prince* which was being built on the Clyde. One great problem for the builders was that a major fire enveloped the Middlesex yard and delayed all the building activities on the site. Much machinery, including a 60hp steam engine was destroyed. Another casualty was that between £10,000-£15,000 of teak, mahogany and oak was destroyed in the fire which could be seen from eight to ten miles away. One immediate result of the damage was that out of the 2,000 to 3,000 men that worked for Thames, no less than 500 were thrown out of work. [16]

However, the *Warrior* was launched on 29th December 1860 which marked the beginning of the modern British screw fleet. With the delays and changes to specifications the ship did not generate a profit for the Thames Iron Works. The eventual cost of the ship to the Admiralty was £357,291 with the Thames Iron Works losing £61,400 on their part of the contract. [17] Despite the loss, the company saw the benefits of the contract through the numerous persons of note that visited their shipbuilding yard. Distinguished visitors that inspected the shipbuilding concern included Grand Duke Constantine, Prince Frederic Wilheim of Germany, the Duke of Cambridge, Lords of the Admiralty and many naval attachés from foreign embassies. This produced many orders for large ships for the navies of Russia, Turkey, Germany, Spain, Portugal, Greece and Denmark. Many of these ships were armour-clad naval vessels. The increase of orders after the building of *Warrior* was spectacular. In late 1861 the yard received orders for two Danish gunboats. In 1863 they were building *Pervenetz*, Russia's

first armour-clad warship; *Vitoria*, for many years the flagship of the Spanish navy, a Turkish frigate and a yacht for the Sultan of Turkey. At this time Thames was also building HMS *Minotaur*. This ship was 400 feet in length which was longer than *Warrior*. The increase in orders meant a further development of the facilities of the Thames Iron Works. According to Barry the works doubled in area. The works was still divided into its two sections along the Bow Creek. The Middlesex side consisted of five acres that contained offices, plumbers, shops and timber yards. On the opposite Essex side was the main yard consisting of 20 acres of slips and buildings. There were eight slips and the largest one could take a ship of 12,000 tons. Patrick Barry inspected the works and deals with the yard in details in his publication, *Dockyard Economy and Naval Power* (1863). [18] In this volume several early photographs of the works were to appear but a dispute broke out with Captain John Ford, the managing director of the Thames Iron Works Company. The photographs were withdrawn from

HMS Warrior, 1860, *built by the Thames Iron Works and photographed in its present preserved state at Portsmouth.*

The size of marine steam engines is clearly shown in this photograph taken in 1862 at the London International Exhibition. These engines were manufactured by Maudslay, Sons & Field and John Penn & Son. Both these firms supplied engines to ships built by the Thames Iron Works.

the book. The book was praising the activities of the private shipbuilding companies and compared them with the inefficiencies of the Royal Naval Dockyards. Ford believed that the criticism of the iron shipbuilding efforts of the government yards was scurrilous. The photographs were not printed for the book and the Thames Iron Works refused to buy any copies. However, before the row Barry had access to the yard and recorded many details about the shipbuilding activities of the Thames Iron Works. The company believed that each year it could build 25,000 tons of iron-clad ships and 10,000 tons of first class merchant steamers. If the yard was pushed then with extra hours of work the total tonnage could be raised to 40,000 tons. It was thought that the Thames Iron Works could be relied on to produce 20,000 tons of iron-clad ships at £50 a ton then this would result in the production of a payment of £1,000,000. Barry seems to feel that these estimates were a little ambitious and that 40,000 tons of iron-clad ships would be produced in two and a half years. Certainly the works had the capacity to build several ships at once. They operated seven slipways. In one area of the works there were three slips, one was 370 feet long, and two others were 400 feet long. Higher up on their property were five more slips of 345 feet, 400 feet, 320 feet, 240 feet and 314 feet. Between the slips were the main workshops of the yard. The Thames Iron Works was also well placed for transport facilities; there was access to the city through the Blackwall Railway, the works was in sight of Brunswick Pier and the Victoria Dock. Added to this was the fact that the North Woolwich Railway skirted the company's forges and smithies at the back. Sidings from the works communicated with this railway allowing access to the Eastern Counties Railway. Barry thought that this was an important point for the works had easy access to coal and iron when compared with the Royal Dockyards in the south of England. It might have been an advantage then but was a problem later in the company's history as shipbuilding migrated closer to the areas that produced coal, iron and steel in Britain. One of the great advantages that Barry saw at the Thames Iron Works was that the works made their own iron out of scrap. The works kept a large reserve of scrap iron so shipbuilding activities were not delayed by waiting for deliveries of iron plate. The Thames Iron Works was known as a manufacturer of iron as well as shipbuilders. The scrap iron was made into plates and angle iron using three powerful rolling mills. The works also used seven large steam hammers in their manufacturing processes. The Thames Iron Works unlike the neighbouring Millwall Ironworks did not have the capacity to produce their own steam engines, and these were mainly ordered from Maudslays or John Penn, both London firms.

It could be that the coldness between Barry and Ford was partly generated by serious problems facing the Thames Iron Works. Perhaps the works had expanded too quickly for in 1863 the company was *'in an exceedingly critical position'* with liabilities of £178,904 greater than the share capital of £150,000. [19] A complete reformation of the concern was called for and in 1864 a new company, the Thames Iron Works, Shipbuilding, Engineering and Dry Dock Co. Ltd was launched.

Konig Wilhelm, an ironclad naval ship built by the Thames Iron Works for the Prussian government in 1869. Here it is photographed in the early twentieth century in its later role as a training ship.

SS Dahabieh built for service on the River Nile in 1870.

CHAPTER FIVE

THE THAMES IRON WORKS, SHIPBUILDING, ENGINEERING AND DRY DOCK CO. LTD

The new company was started with shares of £100 which were far more negotiable and more easily transferable between investors. By 1866 there were about 190 shareholders. Peter Rolt held 237 shares and twelve others held over 100 shares. The directors of the new company were Peter Rolt (Chairman), Captain John Ford (Managing Director), Lord Alan Spencer Churchill, Frank Clarke Hills, William Jackson and John Margetson. The shareholders had contributed near to £400,000 to the formation of the new company. The old assets of the company had been given a valuation of £275,000 which was purchased for £150,000 in shares with the remainder in debentures.

The title of the new company certainly gives us a clue of how the Thames Iron Works was going to be developed. The company would diversify into ship repairing and attempt to increase their engineering contracts. The newly raised money was invested in building two dry-docks, *'at a cost of over a quarter of a million pounds, the bigger one capable of taking any ship afloat'*. [20] At this time there were no dry-docking facilities for large ships on the Thames. Often ships were sent from the Thames for repairs at Southampton or the Mersey. Money was also invested in a general expansion of the works with the purchase of a further eight acres of land adjoining the works thus increasing the frontage of the Thames Iron Works on the river. At this time the works was employing five to six thousand men as business began to pick up.

The Thames Iron Works motto was 'no work no pay' and the firm did not use the gang-contract system that operated in many Thames yards. Although this saved on costs the works did pay a slightly higher official wage than their competitors. This allowed the company to employ the best of the shipbuilders on the Thames. One of the yard's important customers was the Peninsular & Oriental shipping line but after 1865 this market disappeared. Several reasons for this occurrence included the problem over the intended succession of Captain Ford as managing director of the Thames Iron Works and the Peninsular & Oriental's placement of further ship orders in Scotland.

The management of the shipping company had changed with a larger proportion of Scottish directors being elected onto the board. After this date no large commercial ships were built by the company. It was a difficult time for all the Thames builders and the Thames Iron Works had to reduce their work force from 6,000 to 2,000. For the large contracts the works had to rely on securing naval orders from Britain and abroad. [21]

The building of warships was a trade fraught with difficulties. One illustration of these problems was the building by the Thames Iron Works of the 9,600 ton iron-clad *Fatikh* for the Turkish government who later defaulted on payment. It was great relief when Prussia stepped in and purchased the ship and it was renamed *Konig Wilhelm*. At this time this was the only ship to be seen on the slips. This and other foreign naval contracts kept the yard going with the civil engineering division securing a large contract to construct an arched bridge at Blackfriars.

Frank Clarke Hills, a manufacturing chemist from Deptford who was the first member of the family to beocome involved with the Thames Iron Works

In 1867 it was further decided to reduce their commitment to the works on the Middlesex side by reducing the size of the yard and only taking out an annual renewable lease.

During the 1870s commercial shipbuilding by the Thames Iron Works remained low and the ships built there were mainly tugs and small paddle steamers. The company's main naval architect could comment that after putting in many bids for contracts it was the price that, *'led to our being ruled out, as the North Country and the Clyde were making rapid strides, putting down new machinery and doing their utmost to economise on labour'*. The works was in a depressed state but would be invigorated when naval contracts were secured.

In 1873 the Thames Iron Works was building HMS *Rover*, the *Mesoudiye* and *Castalia* and the works looked *'pretty busy again'*. To get any commercial orders specialist ship contracts had to be bid for but this could not lead to further high volume work. In 1877 a comment was made that the *'slips were woefully bare'*. [22] Thames Iron Works was now dependent on its naval contracts. During the 1870s the only large ships built by the Thames Iron Works were for navies and they completed three for the Turkish government, three for Britain and one for Portugal. Even some of the other smaller ships were of a naval character as they built a troopship for Brazil, a torpedo boat for Germany, a torpedo boat for Greece and a troopship and mine layer for Portugal. The only ship built by Thames of over a thousand tons was the *Castalia*.

The other ships completed by the yard consisted of about 29 smaller vessels including customs and tug boats. At the beginning of 1879 activity at the yard was described as *'about as low as could be'*. [23] In 1880 two composite gunboats were completed for the British navy, these were HMS *Swift* and HMS *Linnet* but the difficulties of relying on naval orders can be illustrated by the ordering of a warship for the Peruvian government. This project was terminated when Peru ceased to be at war with Chile. The Thames company was described by their chief naval architect as *'still among the shallows and in constant fear of grounding'*. The management of the Thames Iron Works continued to pursue naval orders although it was a difficult trade.

On one contract the company gained it even though their tender was higher than other firms. They gained the contract by agreeing to time penalties of £100 a day if the construction of the ship went over four months which was the agreed completion date. The contract was signed in October 1880 and the company's naval architect had a fitful night's sleep. He stated that he, *'went to bed but not to sleep, the heavy penalties becoming a nightmare, as the vessels were not large and the profit but small and a few days default would swallow up the profits. Still we wanted work badly as the forge and rolling mills were all but idle and our workmen were in great need'*. To complete the contract the Christmas break had to be reduced to three days and another boat had to be launched in a snow storm to clear the way for the other launch. However, the contract was duly completed on time. [24]

The 1880s at the Thames Iron Works followed the pattern of the 1870s with the building of a series of smaller vessels punctuated by a large naval order that revived the works. In 1881 two cruisers were completed for Spain, they were the *Gravina* and *Velasco*. The early 1880s saw two British battleships being built by the Thames Iron Works. In September 1882 HMS *Benbow* was ordered to be built at the works. This ship was completed in 1885 and HMS *Sans Pareil* was completed in 1887. The building of large naval ships was a good advert for the yard. It attracted dignitaries and naval attachés to inspect the ships and hopefully this would initiate further naval orders. The political machinations of building naval ships could also bring trouble to any yard building these vessels. An example of this is clearly seen in work taken on by the Thames Iron Works in the mid-1880s. Two merchant ships had been built in Germany for Portugal. The government of Peru bought the ships at the German yard and they planned to turn them into naval ships. Chile was at this time at war with Peru and an embargo was placed on the vessels until the end of the war. In 1885, after the war, they were brought to the Thames Iron Works for conversion to naval ships, which included some general modernisation to the vessels. The two ships were at first, named *Diogenes* and *Socrates*. When the conversion of the *Diogenes* was completed it was renamed *Lima* but the payment for the work was that the Thames Iron Works kept *Socrates*. This was later sold to the United States of America and was renamed *Topeka*.

The earlier difficulties of the 1870s can be easily seen in the changes and ownership of the company. In 1871 the company became the Thames Ship Building Graving Docks and Iron Works Co. Ltd which was valued at £250,000. Then in May 1872 the business was renamed the Thames Iron Works and Shipbuilding Co. Ltd. By the early 1870s the management of the company was moving towards the Hills family. Frank C. Hills was a successful manufacturing chemist from Deptford and he had a large stake in the Thames Company owning £100,000 in shares and £97,000 in their debentures. [25]

In May 1873 there were eight shareholders in the Thames Iron Works. Lord Churchill, John Bulmer and six members of the Hills family. In 1880 Arnold Hills joined the Thames Iron Works and was to have an important role in guiding the company into the twentieth century. He was one of Frank Hill's sons and had been educated at Harrow and Oxford University. He was an athlete of note having won the English Mile and had represented the University at football. Arnold Hills was twenty-three when he joined the board and during the 1880s he soon witnessed the highs and lows of the shipbuilding trade on the Thames.

In the 1880s the works built two large ships for the Royal Navy and two gunboats. Two cruisers were completed for the Spanish Government but all the other naval orders were for small ships such as mine layers. During this period about 61 of these smaller ships were completed by the Thames Iron Works. The only fairly large commercial order was the *Invicta* of just over 12,000 tons built for the London, Chatham & Dover Railway Company.

A typical advert showing the shipbuilding skills of the Thames Iron Works. The advert dates to 1896 and shows the main vessels built by the company.

Izzeddin, *a steam paddle yacht built by the Thames Iron Works for the Sultan of Turkey, 1863.*

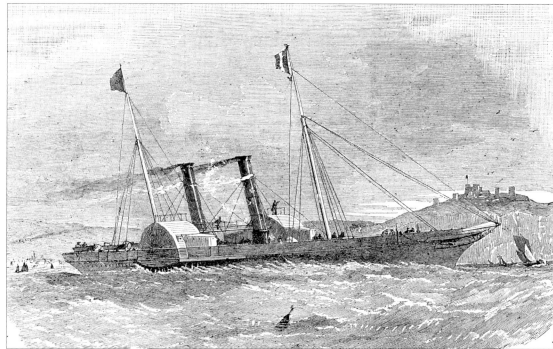

CHAPTER SIX

ARNOLD HILLS AND THE THAMES IRON WORKS

The previous dependence on naval orders by the Thames Iron Works continued during the 1880s and 1890s and during this time 75 per cent of output in tonnage consisted of ships for the Royal Navy. Only a very small percentage of output consisted of work for commercial companies. From 1889 to 1912 the yard built eight large ships for the Royal Navy. These were four cruisers and four battleships. The Thames Iron Works had to win these contracts in competition against shipbuilders situated close to the coalfields. The shipbuilders of the North East and Clydeside had access to cheaper iron, steel and coal plus labour costs were lower. The management at Thames thought that it was important to gain orders from the Admiralty for large ships as this would be a good advert to attract naval orders from foreign governments. However, this strategy seems to have had a declining pull as only two large naval ships were built by the yard for export. These were the Japanese battleships, *Fuji* (1896) and *Shikishima* (1898). British naval orders were so important that when one was obtained the works had a long-standing tradition of running up a flag to let the local population know.

The Thames Iron Works built excellent ships with highly skilled workers but the yard's prices were higher than their competitors. It was thought that Thames had to pay wages to its workers which were 15 to 20 per cent higher than in other British shipbuilding areas. As the works depended on orders from the British Navy the management began to examine the 'fair wage' clauses in British Admiralty contracts. There were changes made in the wording of naval contracts which led to a conference of local authorities at Limehouse. Arnold Hills felt that the government should make allowances for the differing wage rates around Britain when awarding contracts to build naval ships. The Admiralty tenders from the Thames Iron Works were on average 10 per cent higher than the other major British shipbuilders. A Parliamentary Select Committee was set up in 1897 to look into this problem but no changes were made after they finished their deliberations. By this time Arnold Hills was the managing director of the works. He was a man of high principles and fascinating interests. He was a vegetarian and had also founded a number of temperance societies. He wanted to know and understand the problems faced by his workers and for five years lived in East India Dock Road, fairly close to the works. His view did not always agree with those of his employees. He backed the managers' views that the Thames Iron Works had the right to engage non-union men. This led to friction between the management and the workers. The boilermakers went on strike from 9th July to 29th October, the labourers were on strike in August, the joiners

Arnold Hills (1857-1927) who became a director of the company in 1880 and then rose to be the chairman of the concern.

A paddle wheel vessel for Brahmaputra River under construction at the Thames Iron Works in the early 1880s. This was one of four paddle steamers completed for this company in 1882.

were on strike between March until 23rd June 1890, the engineers for three weeks in August 1891 and the shipwrights were on strike for eighteen months from 24th November 1892. Outside the works bands played 'The Dead March', and Hills was jeered at by his own workers when he entered the yard. This disrupted production but replacement workers were found with some non-union men being lodged on a cruiser which was in their mud dock. [26]

Arnold Hills felt that there must be an alternate way with regard to labour relations. He proposed to his board a profit sharing scheme in which 10 per cent of the firm's profits each year were put in a fund to be paid to the workers in addition to their wages. The board of the Thames Iron Works were not impressed by his ideas. Hills resigned but the board did not accept his resignation. However, when the workers were balloted they rejected the scheme. Hills was determined to end the conflict with his workers and in 1892 he successfully introduced a 'Good Fellowship Scheme'. Two years later a standard working day of eight hours was introduced by the Thames Iron Works. Arnold Hills explained his idea of 'Good Fellowship' in the following terms:

(1) The first principle is Unity. Without unity no undertaking can prosper; a house divided against itself must fall.
(2) The second principle is that of Individual Interest. A dead level of fixed daily rates without premium and without profit tend to general stagnation and apathy.
(3) The third principle is Profit. There can be no doubt that good workmen, well led and well organised, can command large profits. Almost every job that comes into the yard, if properly handled, might return to the workman more than the daily rates upon which his week's wages are based. Good workmen and good wages stand to each other in the relation of cause and effect; good wages attract good workmen, and good workmen make the profits from which good wages can be paid.

(4) The fourth principle is profit-division in proportion to wages paid. All individual bonus payments are liable to charges of partiality and favouritism, and as a rule bear no exact relation to the cost of the job upon which they have been paid.

The introduction of the scheme did seem to neutralise the labour unrest that had been prevalent in the yard before this date. Still there was some frustration within the organisation of 'Good Fellowship'. Extra payments were made from profits but extra wages could also be earned if workers completed a piece of work at a lesser cost than a previously agreed fixed price. However, this could generate frustration as often men worked in groups and were dependent on each other. So gains by workers could be neutralised by the less productive work of their colleagues.

The 'Good Fellowship' scheme up to the major reorganisation of the company in 1899 gave the following dividend payments to the workers with the total wage bill in brackets, 1893 - £2,503 (£99,066), 1894 - £1,112 (£102,456), 1895 - £5,852 (£147,790), 1896 - £5,081 (£163,666), 1897 - £7,774 (£223,902), 1898 - £15,390 (£242,838) and 1899 - £13,135 (£279,115).

Arnold Hills wanted to create a family atmosphere within his work force. He spent a large sum

The dignitaries at the laying down of the Portuguese ship Alfonso D'Albuquerque, *c1882. The man holding a hammer, third from left is George C. Mackrow the famous naval architect of the Thames Iron Works.*

on founding clubs at the Thames Iron Works. These included a temperance league, cycling club, athletic club, cricket club, literary club, drama society, tennis club, a choral society, a horticultural society and a works brass military band. One of the most famous of the Thames Iron Works sporting teams was the Thames Iron Works Football Club which won the West Ham Charity Cup and topped the London League. Hills was proud of the endeavours of the works' football team as he was a keen footballer. However, when further progress by the team could only be achieved within a

professional framework, he broke the link between yard and team. The development of the clubs and societies tended to be a difficult struggle as many were formed only to flourish for a brief time before dissolution. Hills also introduced a works magazine. *The Thames Iron Works Quarterly Gazette* was published mainly during the period 1895-1906. It was hoped that this periodical would be, *'a means of friendly communications between our shareholders, our staff, our workmen and myself'*. The magazine contained news about developments within the yard, reports concerning output, notes concerning the social clubs and general articles usually with an engineering bias. During the 1890s the Thames Iron Works built for the Royal Navy three first class cruisers (*Blenheim, Grafton & Theseus*), a destroyer (*Zebra*) and a battleship (*Albion*). The strategy in making every effort to acquire Admiralty contracts was that the management of the yard felt that this would attract further orders from foreign navies. However, only two large orders were generated by this method and these were two battleships for the Imperial Japanese Navy (1896 *Fuji* & 1898 *Shikishima*). During this decade apart from naval ships the other ships built by the company were of a small individual tonnage. However, often historians commenting on the progress of the Thames Iron Works seem to ignore the fact that the company had two other important departments. These were ship repairing and civil engineering. The civil engineering department produced many important products using iron and steel. These included

The Thames Iron Works Football Team, 1896. Later the team turned professional and became West Ham United.

piers, bridges, dock gates, lighthouses and structural ironwork. The ownership of the shares of the Thames Iron Works during the 1890s was dominated by Arnold Hills. Even with the slips not totally occupied by large ships the shipyard was becoming crowded and cramped. In 1898 a large crowd of 20,000 turned up to see the launching of HMS *Albion*. The crowd filled the banks of the river and many found vantage points in parts of the yard. When the ship was launched it created a large wave which broke a workman's bridge on another slipway which threw over two hundred people into the water with around forty drowning.

The building in the 1890s of four large British naval ships and two battleships for Japan must have encouraged the board of the Thames Iron Works to consider expansion. In May 1899 the Thames Iron Works took over the firm of John Penn & Sons. A new public company, the Thames Iron Works,

The Thames Iron Works Operatic Society in the Pirates of Penzance, 1896.

Shipbuilding and Engineering Co. Ltd was set up to take over the assets of the two companies. The new company had the original Thames share capital of £300,000 and moved to raise more capital using non-voting 5 per cent preference shares and 4 per cent debenture capital. The Thames Iron Works had started to expand into building marine engines but with the acquisition of the Penn works, it could now construct all the machinery needed for the ships that they were building. However, they still did not have the capability of producing their own armaments. This put them at a great disadvantage compared with some of the northern yards who could build ships and equip them with their own in-house machinery and armaments. The Penn business had been bought by the old Thames Iron Works Company a week before the new company was formed. Hambros, the banker who was handling the share issue was unhappy at the suggested new capital of the company being set at £600,000. The old company had a capital of £300,000 with the Penn's works adding a further £100,000. The bankers felt that the new company with this structure would be watering down their capital and an inadequate return would be made by shareholders. Some of the profit figures quoted in the prospectus for the new company were optimistic. The acquisition of John Penn & Sons proceeded with their premises at Greenwich and Deptford becoming part of the Thames Iron Works. It was decided to modernise and enlarge the workshops and other premises of John Penn. At the first general meeting of the new company on 30th October 1899 it was announced that new boiler shops, machinery and plant were now practically in working order. [27] Additional plant at the old works of John Penn also included a complete set of electrical driving and lighting machinery. It was stated that the new shops for engines and Belleville boiler manufacture were probably the best in the United Kingdom. This marine engineering department was certainly busy at this time for in its shops were being built 10 sets of machinery for 56ft vedette boats, 9 sets of machinery for 40ft steam pinnaces and six sets of Thames Iron Works patent water tube boilers. Also at this time an order for a third set of 1,800ihp battleship engines had come into the works. It was hoped that these orders would keep the new workshops full of profitable work for the next two years at least. Other good news was also flowing into Thames Iron Works for the Japanese battleship, *Shikishima* had successfully completed its trials and achieved a speed a knot faster than the contracted stipulated speed. This coupled with the fact that the Admiralty had ordered from Thames two battleships seemed to indicate that the works could look forward to a busy and productive period. At this meeting it was reported that HMS *Albion* was practically ready but was awaiting the completion of the machinery by other contractors. The two new battleships HMS *Duncan* and HMS *Cornwallis* were beginning to present an imposing appearance in the yard

LEFT : Members of the Thames Iron Works Temperance League, 1896.

BELOW : Photographed at a local track are these members of the Thames Iron Works Cycling Club, 1896.

Officials and members of the Thames Iron Works Cycle and Athletic Clubs at a meeting, 31st August 1901.

and steady progress was being made with their construction. At the same time it was noted that the company's dry dock had been occupied with a special pressure of repairing business. The civil engineering department had also made excellent progress with the considerable contracts in hand. These projects included the manufacture of the Royal Pavilion for the Paris Exhibition which was near to completion. The board, at this time, was made up of A.F. Hills (chairman), William Penn, E.D.L. Harvey and T.H. Hills. This completely positive report of the progress of the company was reduced somewhat in the first annual report of the company covering the year ending December 1899. At this meeting Arnold Hills had to report that:

> *"The non-delivery of HMS Albion remains the unfavourable feature of last year's work. In accordance with our original contracts, we had made arrangements for the completion of the vessel in the month of August last year. The failure of the Engineers and the consequent non-completion of the propelling machinery has dislocated our arrangements, postponed delivery for 10 months and involved the company in serious losses from circumstances beyond our control. The whole matter is under consideration of the Admiralty, but inasmuch as the present situation was quite unseen at the time of the issue of the company's prospectus, I have undertaken to make myself responsible for any loses that may be involved by this most unfortunate delay."* [28]

The problems of a private shipyard building a major British naval ship at this time are clearly illustrated by this incident. The Thames Iron Works had to sub-contract the machinery and armaments to other firms. Any delay in supplying these contracted parts would delay the completion of the ship and it would be the Thames Iron Works that would be financially penalised by the government. The delay in completing HMS *Albion* happened because Maudslay, Sons & Field Ltd who were building the engines had been declared bankrupt. Perhaps in order to counter this problem the marine engine building works of John Penn was added to the Thames Iron Works in 1899. Profits after deductions were announced of just under £44,000. It was also proposed that, *'In view of the magnitude of our present contracts (exceeding £1,500,000 with the Admiralty alone) and the constant increasing business of the Company, the Directors recommend an increase of £100,000 of working capital'*. At a later meeting it was agreed that the company would seek £200,000 by the creation of 6 per cent cumulative preference B shares of £1 each. This was not a successful strategy as at the Special Meeting held by the company on 2nd August 1900 it was announced that these shares had not been subscribed to sufficiently and it was decided to raise £100,000 through 5 per cent second mortgage debentures to rank immediately behind the existing £200,000 5 per cent first mortgage debentures. The construction of large naval ships meant that firms like the Thames Iron Works had to often invest in new plant, materials and initial payments to contractors who would supply parts for the ship. A large naval contract meant that the company had to raise more money from investors. The second annual general meeting of the company was held on 3rd April 1901 when the shareholders could consider the annual report which detailed the progress of the company until the end of December 1900. [29] This reported the successful launch of the battleship HMS

ABOVE : Franks Ernest Hills. He was the brother of Arnold Hills and was the third member of the family to become a director of the company.

LEFT : The general office staff pictured at the Thames Iron Works in 1906.

The Platers Football Team who won the Thames Iron Works Trades Football Shield in the season 1900 – 1901.

Duncan. The yard during the year also built a number of barges, small craft and twenty lifeboats. The Thames Iron Works was justly proud of their boat-building department. Five years previously they started to build lifeboats and within three years had impressed the members of the board of the Royal National Lifeboat Institution with the quality of their output. The Thames Iron Works was then invited to undertake the entire construction, equipment and repair of their lifeboat fleet. During the previous two years this department had turned out forty lifeboats. The marine engineering works at Greenwich had also been busy during the year. Under the managership of George S. Young the machinery and boilers for HMS *Duncan, Cornwallis* and *Albemarle* together with twenty sets of smaller machinery had been completed. The civil engineering department had also had an excellent year with contracts completed for India, Syria, Australia and South Africa. It was also stated that the dry docks had as usual been busy throughout the year. It was believed that every one of the large departments had made substantial profits. At this juncture the board of the Thames Iron Works had to be altered. William Penn withdrew through illness and the Reverend E.D.L. Harvey had to resign because he was technically disqualified as a Clerk in Holy Orders. They were replaced by William Longstaff Ainslie and George Scholey Young. Young was the works manager at the marine engineering department at Greenwich. This was one of the weaknesses of the organisation of the Thames Iron Works. The Hills family owned the major percentage of the shares in the company and it would have been difficult to attract a director for the company from the remaining shareholders. So a company manager was voted on to the board. This method of director recruitment continued throughout the first decade of the twentieth century which made the board rather introspective and did not allow a fresh perspective to be introduced. The company was still in profit but was reduced

The Thames Iron Works Horticultural Annual Show, 1906. Arnold Hills is pictured in the foreground.

from the previous year. The profit was calculated at around £39,500 but after deductions there was £34,473 that could be distributed. The annual report for the year ending December 1901 could only record the situation at the works as steady and is a much shorter document. [30] The featured work in the text is a description of some contracts undertaken by the civil engineering department. Here was being constructed large caissons for the new docks at Gibraltar and at Keyham, Plymouth. It was thought that the building of these caissons would occupy the civil engineering department for two years. Profits were recorded but one dissenting voice was heard at the meeting. One shareholder had noticed that no depreciation had been allowed in the accounts on buildings and fixed plant. It was suggested that the payment of the 5 per cent cumulative preference interest for the past half year be postponed and the sum of £7,500 be applied writing off as much depreciation as possible. The motion was lost. The number of directors was now down to three and were Arnold Hills, T.H. Hills and W.L. Ainslie for George S. Young who had been the manager for eleven years at Greenwich had died in February.

The pursuit of British navy contracts continued during the early 1900s but gaining such work became very difficult for the Thames Iron Works. It was true that they had improved their chances of contracts by being able to build their own engines but other factors were working against the company. At one time the Thames Iron Works was able to produce their own iron from scrap for shipbuilding. This could no longer service the building of what had become very large ships. Naval

Repair work at the dry dock of the Thames Iron Works, 1905.

ships in Britain were now being built with the armour plate not of wrought iron but a mixture of iron and steel and later with steel alone. The Thames Iron Works also did not produce their own armaments so both guns and armour plate had to be purchased to build a naval vessel. The iron and steel plate was known as compound armour, two types being Harvey and Krupp armour plate. Steel was now becoming the most important constituent of a naval ship. A firm like Vickers in the northwest made iron and steel, built ships, produced their own armour plate and manufactured guns and armaments. In Scotland several firms combined to try to neutralise what became known as the 'Northern or Armament Ring'. They developed an armaments factory in Coventry to be able to produce their own guns and mountings to be able to compete with firms like Vickers. Another firm also entered the market, this was Sir William G. Armstrong & Co Ltd who had combined the manufacture of ordnance with shipbuilding at Elswick on the Tyne. In 1897 this firm announced its intention of also making armour plate after a merger with Sir Joseph Whitworth & Co. the Manchester engineers. Arnold Hills felt that the 'Northern Ring' firms could put in a low tender for Admiralty

A slipway at the Thames Iron Works being prepared for the construction of a Japanese battleship, 1897.

work because they were not seeking profit from the hull but only from the armaments for the ship. It was a lucrative trade for in 1907-1908 the Admiralty expenditure on gun mountings alone came to £1,825,239. He believed that the government should keep that in mind when awarding tenders for naval ships.

The annual report for the year ending December 1902 bemoaned the fact that no Admiralty contracts had come their way in the early part of the year. [31] However, towards the end of the year the Thames Iron Works was awarded the contract for HMS *Black Prince*, a first class cruiser. It was hoped that this would keep the marine engineering department profitably occupied for the next two or three years for they were also building the 21,000ihp engines for HMS *Devonshire*. One bright naval

development was that the Admiralty had decided to let out some naval repairs to private yards. Over the past twelve months the Thames Iron Works had carried out extensive repairs to HMS *Colossus*, minor repairs to HMS *Gleaner* and had recently received orders for the overhaul of HMS *Crescent*. This work was completed on a cost plus percentage basis so it was one type of British naval work that did not pose any financial risks. Work during this period in the civil engineering department included the caissons for Keyham and Gibraltar and recently completed was three sets of dock gates for the Tredegar Dry Dock at Newport. Other completed work included the steelwork for Folkestone Harbour and a caisson for the Alexandria Dry Dock. Demand for

ABOVE: The ram of the Japanese battleship Fuji *under construction at the Thames Iron Works, c1893.*

RIGHT: The stern of the Japanese battleship Fuji *being built in around 1893.*

Hone's Patent Grab which was manufactured by the works continued well. However, there is a note of disappointment concerning the dry dock department as it had dealt with a considerable tonnage of vessels but with no big repairs. One link with the past ended in 1902 for the leasehold premises at Blackwall was required by the owners. This had been held by the Thames Iron Works on an annual tenancy. So the directors, drawing and office staff were moved to the opposite side of Bow Creek. This ended a 65 year occupancy and also ended the travelling by chain ferry from one side of the works to the other. This journey was often difficult because of the tides and weather and at times the creek was impassable.

One piece of bad news was that the manufacture of the engines and machinery for HMS *Duncan* and HMS *Cornwallis* had produced a loss. The board excused this fact by stating that the estimates had been drawn up by the old firm of John Penn & Sons. The board changed at this juncture with the resignation of W.L. Ainslie and he was replaced by George C. Mackrow, the chief naval architect of the Thames Iron Works. This appears to have been another rather introspective appointment leaving

Workers at the Thames Iron Works disembarking from the ferry that transported them across the river. This service connected the different parts of the works that existed on both sides of the Bow Creek.

RIGHT: The old general office of the Thames Iron Works, Blackwall.

BELOW: The new offices of the Thames Iron Works, photographed in around 1905.

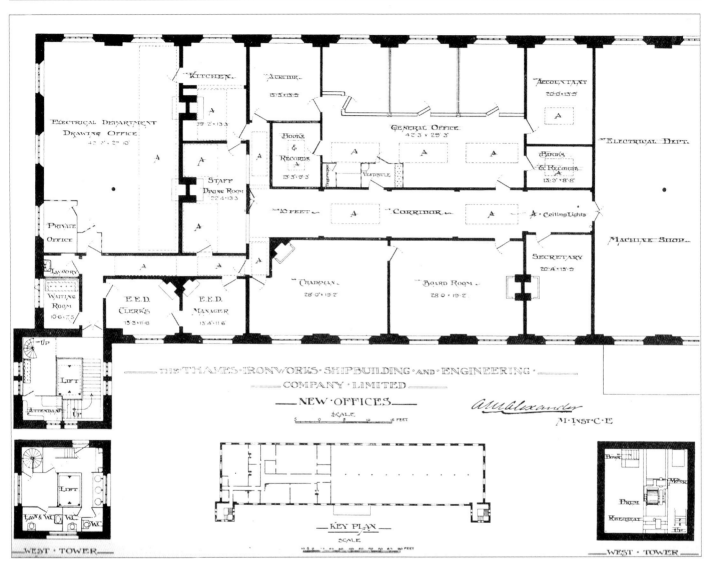

The plan for the new offices of the Thames Iron Works.

the board as Arnold F. Hills, T.H. Hills, A.M. Alexander and G.C. Mackrow. Although profits were announced there was criticism from some quarters because of the low market price of the company's shares. Several historians have examined the progress of the Thames Iron Works through its activities as a shipbuilder. However in the early 1900s the output of the works was of a diverse character. In June 1900 the Thames Iron Works was inspected by members of the Institution of Mechanical Engineers who recorded the following. In the civil engineering department they saw the following products being manufactured, girder work for the Tarkwa Railway in the Gold Coast, steel cement stock boxes and columns, spans of various sizes for the Norwegian Trunk Railways, 30ft spans for the East Indian Railway, steel freezing cells for the Atlas Co. of Copenhagen, spans of various sizes for the

The shipbuilding department foremen photographed at the Thames Iron Works in 1904.

The boardroom of the Thames Iron Works, c1905. Prominently displayed on the left hand side is a large model of HMS Warrior *of 1860.*

Burma Railways, spans of various sizes for the Bengal-Nagpur Railway and various roofing and steel constructional items. In the shipbuilding department they saw HMS *Duncan* and HMS *Cornwallis* being built. In the boat building sheds the party saw a number of lifeboats being constructed for the Royal National Lifeboat Institution and also steel barges for Wm Cory & Son. Also noticed was the dry dock department which had shear legs capable of lifting 80 tons. There were two dry docks, a larger one and a smaller example. The members also inspected the electrical engineering department

The barge built for Queen's College, Oxford by the Thames Iron Works in 1904.

which not only carried out work on the ships under construction but undertook general electrical contracts. Dynamos, motors, electric fans, portable electrical drilling machines, searchlight projectors, switches, and switchboards were manufactured in the machine shops facing the river. A central generating station had been established in the works. This consisted of three locomotive and two gunboat boilers and nine set of engines and dynamos aggregating 350 kw, three of which were built by the Thames Iron Works. [32]

The 5th annual report chronicled the progress of the company up to the end of December 1903. [33] The works must have looked busy for in the shipbuilding department HMS *Black Prince* was being constructed and also in the yard HMS *Colossus* and HMS *Crescent* were being overhauled. *Colossus* was a battleship completed in 1896 and *Crescent* was a first class cruiser completed in 1894. The Thames Iron Works also completed a number of smaller vessels during the year including a 50 ton floating crane for the London and India Docks, three 300 ton coal lighters for the Admiralty, a general service steamboat for the War Office and 13 lifeboats. The marine engineering department for the year could report that they had built the machinery for HMS *Black Prince* and the machinery for HMS *Devonshire*. They had also provided machinery for the refit of HMS *Colossus* and HMS *Crescent*. The department was also providing the cylindrical boilers for HMS *New Zealand* and HMS *Caernarvon*. In the civil engineering department there was also a healthy look about their completed work. The

Nine out of the ten steamboats under construction for the London County Council. The Thames Iron works were able to build these ships without using a slipway, c1904.

twelve floating caissons had been finished for the Admiralty. Another order had also come to the department for a floating caisson for the new dock at Hong Kong. The chairman felt that the benefits of the 'Good Fellowship' scheme was beginning to work its way through the organisation. At this meeting T. H. Hills retired from the board and was replaced by David Urquhart MIEE who was the company's electrical engineer. The operating profit for the year ending 31st December 1903 was £34,015, this being the total before deductions. The sixth annual general meeting of the company took place on 12th April 1905. [34] The year ending 31st December 1904 was reviewed with some optimism. The directors (A.F. Hills, A.M. Alexander, G.C. Mackrow & D. Urquhart) could report that they had, *'the pleasure in making what is considered the most satisfactory report of the company's work since*

LEFT: One of the sets of the compound diagonal steam engines built for the London County Council paddle steamers, c1904.

BELOW: George Scholey Young (1850 - 1901). Young was one of the brilliant marine engine designers employed in the later history of the works. His early death in 1901 robbed the works of an experienced mechanical engineer.

its incorporation in 1899'. HMS *Black Prince* had been launched and the London County Council had ordered ten steamboats from the yard. These were for a new River Thames service. The Thames Iron Works was also building a 1,000 coal-bagging lighter and were busy with the construction of a number of lifeboats, pinnaces, lighters and barges. It was considered that it was a record year at the Greenwich marine engineering works.

The company was also developing the manufacture of steam and oil transportation. Soon a range of cars, lorries and buses were produced. There were experiments carried out using both steam and petrol as the motive power. The one disappointing result was from the dry dock department. It was reported that this part of the company had suffered with their rivals from the severe depression during the last eighteen months. The declared operating profits were £52,633 which after deductions became £34,392. The following year's report was also pretty positive although there was a note of caution as the chairman stated *'we were not fortunate in securing any contracts of importance from the Admiralty'.* However, an order for eight torpedo vedette boats had come in from the Romanian government. The civil engineering department had completed a considerable amount of general work such as dock gates, piers and bridges for India, Japan and other countries. An operating profit of £64,498 was declared and after deductions there was a

profit of £34,392. There was gloom in the annual report for the year ending 31st December 1906 for no new Admiralty contracts had come the way of the Thames Iron Works. [35] Only one contract for a battleship of the Dreadnought type had been given out. It was now believed that the beam of these huge ships would mean that the Thames Iron Works did not have a dock big enough for fitting out these vessels. However, the engineering department was making considerable progress in the manufacture of motor omnibuses, vans and cars. To serve this trade a West End agency and garage had been opened. The civil engineering department had also recently received an order for three pairs of dock gates for the Swansea Harbour Trust. One piece of sad news was recorded in the company's annual report and that was the death of their long serving naval architect, G.C. Mackrow. His place on the board was taken by his son, Clement Mackrow who was yet again another employee of the company. An operating profit of £58,199 was declared and after deductions this was recorded as £53,055.

It was presumed by the board of the Thames Iron Works that 1907 to 1908 was a good opportunity

ABOVE: Clement Mackrow. He was to replace his father as a director and marine architect for the Thames Iron Works in 1906. Clement Mackrow died at the age of fifty seven in 1912 as the works was being closed and the premises vacated.

RIGHT: A completed Orloff colour printing machine photographed in the workshops of the Thames Iron Works, 1902.

for the company to gain contracts from the Admiralty for it was stated that *'This year's naval programme provides for a considerable number of vessels of various classes to be built by contract and we are looking forward with confidence to obtaining our fair share of this work for which we are so well equipped'*. This, certainly, did not happen in 1907. [36] The yard did complete two twin screw passenger ships for Turkey and received news that the eight torpedo vedette boats built by Thames had arrived safely. The works also added another string to their bow by obtaining an order for four large stationary engines for the new pumping station at Walton-on-Thames of the Metropolitan Water Board. These were to be triple expansion engines to a similar design to the engines that the Thames Iron Works built for their large naval ships. John Penn & Sons had built some stationary engines in their early history but had not developed this trade. This was an opportunity for the Thames Iron Works to open up another market for their products. The civil engineering department, at this time, had completed an iron jetty for Accra, a lighthouse for the new Admiralty pier at Dover and various bridges and structural steel work for India. However, during this period the repairing business had been generally very scarce. Much reduced profits were announced and employment within the company had fallen from 3,180 in 1902 to 1,020 in the first half of 1907. The company results for the year ending 31st December 1908 were not good. [37] The board had to announce a loss *because of the prevailing depression of trade and the continued absence of Admiralty orders'*. However, Hills' constant

ABOVE: A.M. Alexander, M. Inst C.E., M.I.N.A. who was the manager of the civil engineering department. He later became the Deputy Chairman of the Thames Iron Works Company in its final years.

LEFT: The rather grand heading of a debenture share certificate issued by the Thames Iron Works in 1910.

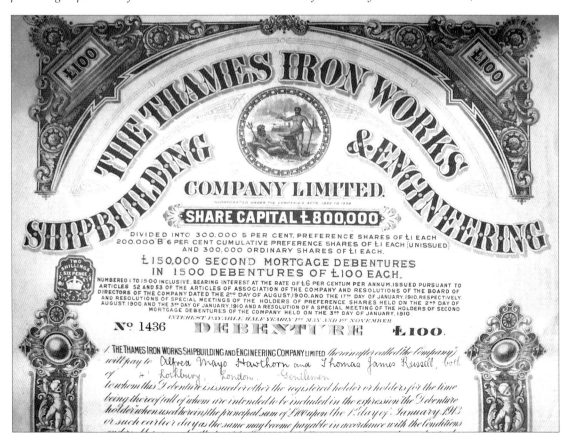

badgering and urging seems to have paid off for there was a belief that an Admiralty order for a first class battleship was coming the way of the Thames Iron Works. But to complete a large naval ship more capital was needed. Each new design of battleship was radically different to its predecessors. New capital was needed to re-tool and to develop new equipment. The earlier battleships that the company had built were equipped with triple expansion steam engines but now the Thames Iron Works had to build one with Parsons steam turbines The Admiralty was not pleased that the Thames Iron Works could not complete the ship at their works and for fitting out the company had to develop a new finishing berth at Dagenham. This also needed a new 150 ton floating crane and special plant at Canning Town and Greenwich. The new money raised could only help the yard continue if further orders for large ships came their way from the Admiralty. As an added complication Arnold Hills' health was in a serious decline. The contract awarded was to build HMS *Thunderer* and the vessel had to be completed in the short space of two years. This would add extra expense for it would mean a system of day and night work. For the year ending December 1909 a final loss of £15,800 was announced. Robert Warriner, who was the company's chief

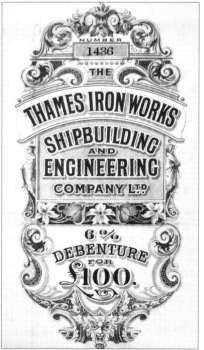

ABOVE: An engraving of a paddle steamer built by the Thames Iron Works for a Turkish company.

RIGHT: A detail of a share certificate issued by the Thames Iron Works.

marine engineer was added to the board. [38] The company's annual report for the year ending 31st December 1910 certainly contains a hint of optimism. [39] In it is recorded that the, *'tide of industrial depression, so far as the Thames Iron Works is concerned, has now turned and the prospects seem bright for a recurrence of more prosperous years'.* However, no profits were declared for the year. One worrying note was that the capital expenditure involved in the construction of HMS *Thunderer* had meant a further issue of debentures to provide for the increased costs. It was also noted that, *'As HMS Thunderer is nearly 50 per cent larger than HMS Duncan and HMS Cornwallis for both we were given 36 months as our time for completion, it will be realized that we undertook a very heavy task in guaranteeing the completion of the vessel in the abnormally short period of two years.'* The general works remained busy during the year. The civil engineering department had completed an iron jetty for Lagos Harbour, bridges for South African railways, iron and steel work for the Tanjong Pagar Wharf and a pontoon for a 150 ton floating crane. Work in progress also included two large floating caissons for the new graving dock

The trade stand of the Thames Iron Works at the Paris Exhibition of 1900.

The Thames Iron Works exhibit at the fourth motor exhibition at Olympia, 1906. The company's exhibit included a steam lorry designed to carry 4 tons, a 15cwt petrol delivery van and a 24/30 bhp motor omnibus chassis.

at Singapore, dock gates for HM Dockyard, Devonport and bridgework for India. At Greenwich the machinery for HMS *Nautilus*, a torpedo boat destroyer was being fitted and also being built there was the machinery for HMS *Thunderer* and the first class cruiser HMS *Chatham*. During the year the dry dock department had been short of work in the first six months but matters improved in the next six months with the principal contract being for the repair of a French railway ship which occupied the large dry dock for two months. It was at this juncture that Clement Mackrow resigned from the board of the company. One bright note was the successful launch of HMS *Thunderer* which took place on 1st February 1911. This impressive 'Orion' class Super-Dreadnought battleship was named and launched by Mrs Randall Davidson the wife of the Archbishop of Canterbury. It was thought by Hills that this would be the beginning of a new chapter in the history of the Thames Iron Works. The works' journal, *The Thames Ironworks Gazette* had been resurrected for 1911 with a new stylish design.

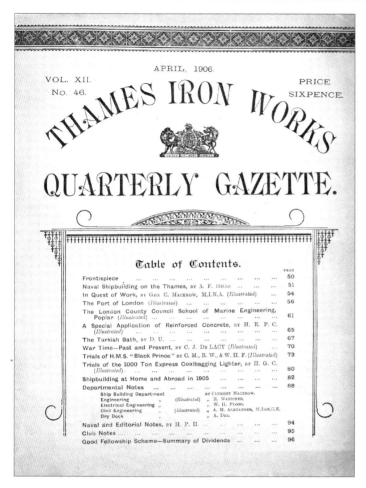

VOL. XII.
No. 46.
APRIL, 1906.
PRICE
SIXPENCE.

THAMES IRON WORKS QUARTERLY GAZETTE.

Table of Contents.

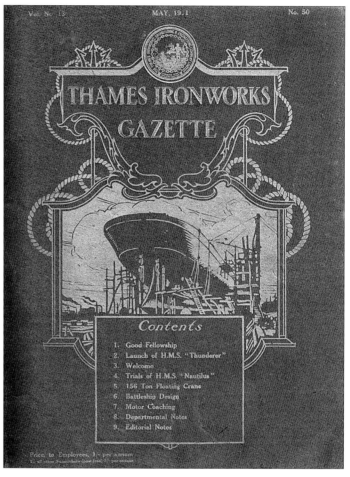

Vol. No. 13 MAY, 1911 No. 50

THAMES IRONWORKS GAZETTE

Contents

Price, to Employees, 1/- per annum

Hills in the February edition explains that the Gazette had not been published for three years because of his rheumatism. It was more likely a cost cutting exercise during the lean years of the yard.

At the meal after the launch of HMS *Thunderer* and in the 1911 editions of the Gazette, Hills continually criticised the Admiralty for not giving more orders to the Thames. Each photograph of the launch of HMS *Thunderer* in the May edition of the Gazette includes a barbed comment such as, '*The Admiralty for years declared a Dreadnought could not be launched on the Thames*', or '*The Admiralty have ignored the Thames and refused their lowest tendered prices on more than 20 occasions – Londoners, is this fair play?*' This strategy produced no further results.

The building of HMS *Thunderer* had financially crippled the company, there was no way back. An examination of the minute book of the Thames Iron Works now tells of a sharp decline. From June 1911 the hand writing is scruffy and difficult to read. The annual reports also become shorter and so less detailed.

Since the middle of November 1911 banks had declined to honour the company's cheques and the firm was being run by a receiver-manager, a Mr F.B. Smart. Arnold Hills was adept at putting pressure on the British government and mobilising public opinion regarding the Thames Iron Works. A march

ABOVE LEFT: The rather utilitarian front cover of the Thames Iron Works gazette. This cover was produced for a 1906 edition of the magazine and was the format adopted for the majority of the issues.
ABOVE RIGHT: The more dynamic cover of the Thames Iron Works Gazette for 1911. Revived to coincide with the completion of HMS Thunderer in that year.

was organised on 1st January 1912 from the East End to Trafalgar Square in which 10,000 people took part in. The object of the demonstration was, *'to demand the right of East London to participate in the building of the British Navy'*. There were rumours of a takeover by another yard with contracts for two cruisers being offered. However, the labour force at Thames was used to working an eight hour day and this put off any other yards being interested. No buyers came forward and the contracts for the two cruisers were given to the Royal Dockyards.

On 21st December 1912 the Thames Iron Works was closed with the clerical staff being given fourteen days' notice and making redundant the remaining 800 workers. Arnold Hills kept trying to resurrect the works through a reconstruction fund of £100,000 but to no avail. The Canning Town site was sold in May 1913 to the Great Eastern Railway Company for £145,000 and the former Penn works at Greenwich was sold to Messrs Defries, an engineering company from Deptford. It was said that much excellent shipbuilding machinery owned by the Thames Iron Works was sold at scrap prices. As the works was dismantled Hills would remind observers that 'no Thames Iron Works built ship has ever yet gone down at sea'. This was not strictly true as *Charkieh* built at the Thames

BELOW LEFT :
Mrs Arnold Hills photographed helping to lay the keel of HMS Thunderer, *16th April 1910.*

BELOW RIGHT:
Mr Arnold Hills in his ambulance chair at the laying of the keel of HMS Thunderer, *1910.*

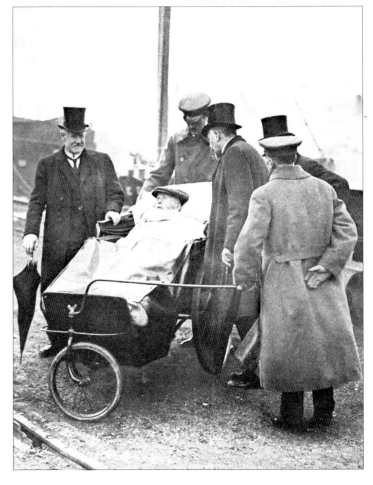

LEFT: The 150 ton crane that had to be built by the company to help fit out HMS Thunderer.

BELOW: The new additional works being built by the Thames Iron Works at Dagenham. This was being built in 1911 to aid the fitting out of HMS Thunderer.

Iron Works in 1865 sank in 1900, *Ly-ee-Moon* built in 1859 sank in 1886 and *Ville du Havre* (built as *Napoleon III*) sank in 1873. However, for the large number of ships built by the Thames Iron Works this represents an incredibly low percentage of losses and Hills could be proud of this.

Many of the early historic engineering works closed during the late nineteenth and early twentieth centuries. These works were often in difficult, constrained situations and expansion was difficult to maintain. Very often they were labouring with old fashioned equipment and lack of investment. The Neath Abbey Ironworks closed in 1890, the Perran Foundry in Cornwall closed in 1879 and Harvey & Co. of Hayle ceased building engines and other engineering products in 1903. [40] This was a pattern repeated with regard to engineering along the Thames. Maudslay Sons & Field became insolvent in 1899 and many other similar works along the Thames went out of business at the same time. In 1907 Humphrys, Tennant & Co. announced the closure of their works at Deptford Pier, blaming this on higher wages that had to be paid in London area, the higher cost of coal and materials and the much higher rates in London especially the rating of machinery. So another major builder of marine engines on the Thames was forced into closure. The Thames Iron Works was labouring under these high costs of raw materials. Ships made from iron and steel could be built at much lower costs at

HMS Thunderer *starts to move down the slipway during the launch.*

works that were nearer to the coalfields and works that made iron and steel. These areas that had this advantage were the Scottish works along the Clyde, Barrow in Furness and the Tyne works in the North-East of England. If the management of the Thames Iron Works had reduced their ambitions slightly then the works could have continued for some years with a much smaller output.

In the early twentieth century the works had introduced some interesting and modern products to their output. They had an electrical manufacturing department, the works built early examples of cars and lorries and had even manufactured some components for aircraft. However, Arnold Hills was besotted with the idea of building large capital ships for the Royal Navy. In 1912, on the Thames, this was a dream that had come to an end. There would be no way forward for the Thames Iron Works to build any more Dreadnought type battleships on their property.

The construction of HMS *Thunderer* had stretched the company's skills and capacity to the maximum. This ship was so large that it could not be completed at the shipyard and for fitting out it was taken to Dagenham. These battleships could only get larger and *Thunderer* could only just be

PUNCH, OR THE LONDON CHARIVARI.—FEBRUARY 1, 1911.

A PROUD PARENT.

NEPTUNE. "SHIP AHOY! WHAT SHIP'S THAT?"   FATHER THAMES. "*THUNDERER*. LITTLE THING OF MY OWN."

Punch's view of the launch of the Thunderer *in the 1st February 1911 edition of their magazine*

squeezed onto the largest of the company's slips. The story of the yard ended in December 1912, but what a story and what a fantastic range of ships were built at the yard by a highly skilled workforce. Many of the ships built by the Thames Iron Works were still afloat in the middle of the twentieth century and several are preserved to be seen today.

CHAPTER SEVEN

THE THAMES IRON WORKS IN 1895

The Thames Iron Works was often visited by industrialists, dignitaries and representatives of the technical press. Fortunately the records of one of these visits has been printed in detail. All of the major departments at the Thames Iron Works were visited in 1895. [41] In that year in the civil engineering department were fitting and machine shops, a smithy with steam hammers, the mould loft, press sheds and a large erecting yard. Serving this department were clerical and drawing offices and also the general stores. The drawing office was a lofty well lighted room which was 49ft by 20ft. This office was occupied by fourteen draughtsmen and five clerks. The work of the civil engineering department consisted chiefly of iron bridges, roofs, dock gates, caissons, tanks, buoys, hydraulic and general machinery, grabs and dredgers. The smithy in this department was 117ft by 40ft with eighteen fires driven by a fan with a steam engine. The smithy possessed two steam hammers, one was a 25cwt hammer and the other was a 5cwt example. The area was served by three large traveller

The pattern shop at the Thames Iron Works photographed in 1894

A Thames Iron Works boiler shell drilling machine, 1894.

The large machine shop, Thames Iron Works 1894.

The girder shed and gantry photographed in 1894.

gantries each 250ft by 52ft 9ins. Two of these gantries were worked by steam, one being designed for a load of 30 tons and the other for 5 tons. The third example was an electric one with a lift of 5 tons. There was also present in the yard a fourth gantry worked by hydraulic power. At this time new machines had been added to this department among which were large lathes, planes, slotters, punching, shearing and straightening presses all of the most modern design. This modernisation of the department included the installation of radial drills. The drills were placed in a line down the shop and it was thought that these would double the output of drilled work. One of the new machines put into the press shed was an exceptionally heavy and massive punching and shearing machine of the lever and cam type made by Messrs Bennie & Sons of the Clyde Engine Works of Glasgow. It was capable of punching 1½ins. holes through 1½ins. steel plates at one of its ends and shearing the same thickness of plate at the other. The machine was also fitted with a powerful angle bar cutter at one of its sides. It was driven by its own steam engine.

    Also in this shed by the same maker was an especially strong and powerful beam bending machine of the horizontal type capable of bending beams up to 16ins deep at one end. At the southern end of that department was one of the most useful machines where girder-making was a speciality. This was a multiple drilling and milling machine made for the company by Messrs Joshua Buckton & Co. of Leeds. This machine had a stationary bed 100ft long and 6ft 8ins wide upon which girder plates could be fixed up to a height of 4ft. Also noticed at that time was a combined plate-edge and butt-end plating machine capable of doing a large amount of work by Messrs Loudon Brothers of Glasgow. In the same shop were two powerful machines of the latest design by Messrs Dean, Smith & Grace of Keighley, one being a self-contained double-geared self-acting radial drill. The other tool by this maker was a powerful and substantially built double-geared slotting machine which had been adapted for heavy cutting.

The contract work in hand in this department included a new steel bridge to carry the traffic across the River Lea from the Poplar to the West Ham side, also known as the Barking Road Bridge. Also being constructed at that time were four steel swing bridges for the Isle of Dogs to the order of the London County Council, namely the Preston Road, Limehouse, City Arms and Manchester Road bridges. Other work being manufactured at that time included about 1,000 tons of steel girder work for a bridge on one of the Indian railways.

The activity in the Marine Engineering Department was also related in detail. This must have been a new foundation. This department was then capable of undertaking the construction of the largest size of marine engines and was under the management of Mr G. Young. It comprised large and small machine shops, erecting, fitting, smiths' and boiler shops together with pattern shops and iron and brass foundries. The principal block of this department was 284ft by 190ft. At each end were towers that were 106ft in height from ground level. On the first floor was the drawing office and when busy it contained twenty staff. The building contained many specimens of excellent machine tools such as a large table planning machine by Messrs Joshua Buckton & Co. of Leeds.

Also in this main workshop was a heavy drilling machine by Messrs J Hulse & Co. of Manchester and a milling machine by Muir & Co. of Manchester. There was a second machine shop which was also well equipped. The pattern makers' shop was 86ft by 60ft and had recently been fitted out with entirely new tools and machinery over the last two years. The boiler makers' shop consisted of two

The girder yard and gantry at the Thames Iron Works photographed in 1894.

An eight spindle drilling machine at the Thames Iron Works.

The timber yard at the Thames Iron Works photographed in 1894.

ABOVE LEFT: The old Thames Iron Works naval architect's office photographed in 1894.

ABOVE RIGHT: The new naval architect's office photographed in the early years of the twentieth century.

RIGHT: A milling and copying machine built for the Thames Iron Works by W. Muir & Co. in the 1890s.

bays or spans of 55ft width by 300ft long. Equipment here included a fine set of rolls by Campbells & Hunter of Leeds and drilling machines by the same maker. One interesting machine there was specially designed for the works by Kendall & Gent of Manchester for the purpose of screwing both ends of marine boiler tubes at the same time and it also formed an excellent hollow mandrel lathe for turning heavy studs and bolts from solid bar. The total number of machines in the marine engineering department was 183 and the power for driving them was obtained from a pair of 22ins x 2ft 6ins horizontal high pressure steam engines, a vertical 12ins & 20ins cylinder steam engine with a stoke of 1ft 8ins and one 24ins x 3ft 6ins horizontal high pressure steam engine. The collective driving power of these engines was about 20hp.

The dry dock department received a detailed examination in this report. The repair of ships was under the management of Mr A. Doe. The upper dock was 467ft by 64ft with a draught of water over the sills of 23ft. By 1895 upwards of 5,000,000 tons of shipping had been docked, overhauled, repaired and in many cases renewed in the company's dry dock. Among the many important works carried out in the dry docks was the repair to the Russian cruiser *Zabiaka* which was on its way to the Baltic, new from her builders in Philadelphia. She was run into and had her port quarter completely cut down, the damage extending beyond the middle line which necessitated the removal of nearly the whole of her stern, all of which was removed in a month. Another important contract was the repair of the Dover and Calais mail boat *Invicta*. She was stranded on the French coast and lay rolling there for some three days. The company shored up her machinery and the damaged bottom was cut out and renewed within four weeks. In 1894 the Royal Mail steamer *Dunottar Castle* was repaired by the Thames Iron Works. In dense fog she scraped the Eddystone Rock and on docking was found to require an entire new stern which in sixteen days was fitted to her. The year of 1894 proved to be a record one with regards to the tonnage dealt with in the dry docks. In that year the company

Vertical rolls built for the Thames Iron Works by Campbells & Hunter, engraved in 1894.

An aerial view of the Thames iron Works photographed in the late nineteenth century. The size of the battleships built at the yard is apparent by the vessel in the bottom right hand corner of the picture. On the extreme left can be seen a white vessel, this was the cruiser accepted in part payment for work for the government of Peru. The vessel spent several years in that dock waiting for a buyer.

A plan of the Thames Iron Works in the late 1890s, engraved in 1894.

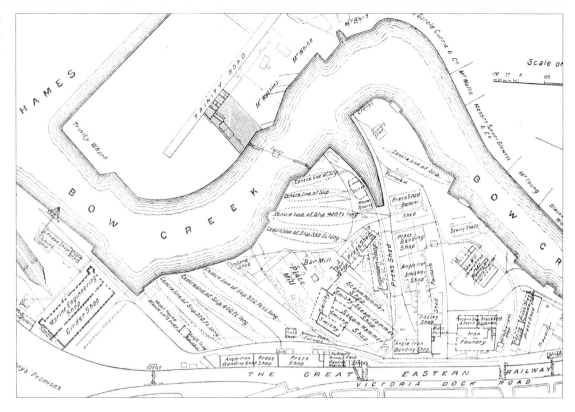

repaired the Peninsular & Oriental Company's steamer *Coromandel* after a collision in the English Channel. The ship's stern and bow plating was renewed in eight days with the work being carried out day and night continuously. The dry docks had shear legs capable of lifting 80 tons deadweight. The second dry dock was smaller measuring 335ft by 46ft with the draught over the sills being 19ft.

The most important part of the Thames Iron Works in 1895 was the shipbuilding department. The workshops there had a frontage of 1,206ft and there were eight building slips. These were of varying lengths of between 200ft to 400ft. At that time only two of the building slips were occupied, although the Russian transport *Samoyed* had lately been launched from another slip. This department had been lately refitted with all modern shipyard tools. In the smiths' shop a large gas furnace had been fitted in conjunction with a 20cwt steam hammer. This was heating iron in half the time taken by an ordinary furnace and with one half the expenditure of fuel. Rails had been laid throughout the yard and five steam cranes were continuously running over these metals. The machinery included six steam hammers, twenty punching presses, sixteen shearing presses, two bar straightening machines, three plate rolls and two plate levellers. The machine tools including the planers were fifty in number. There were five smithies on the yard having eighty hearths, four plate furnaces and six angle bar furnaces. At that time the buildings in the shipyard covered 27,000 square yards and the number of men ordinarily employed in the yard and shops amounted to 1,500. When this report was written the yard was building two ships, namely HMS *Zebra*, a torpedo boat destroyer and the Japanese battleship *Fuji*.

CHAPTER EIGHT

SHIPS BUILT BY THE THAMES IRON WORKS FOR THE ROYAL NAVY

The spread of steam power in Britain during the early nineteenth century did not go unnoticed by the Admiralty. In 1815 the steamship *Congo* started to be constructed for an expedition to the river of the same name. The engine was provided by Boulton & Watt. However, they tried to fit a heavy A frame beam engine to this vessel and the result was that the paddle wheels were pushed too deeply into the water by the weight. Although *Congo* was not a success the Admiralty continued to build and order steam vessels. These ships were built of wood. The early naval ships were paddle steamers and even some wooden frigates were modified to take engines and paddle wheels. The early engine designs were mainly of the side lever type but soon other designs were developed. They included the trunk and Siamese types. The Post Office ordered their first iron hulled ship in 1839. This was the *Dover* and over the next few years the Admiralty compared the running costs of this ship with wooden paddle steamers. There appeared to be no difference in running costs for the two types of vessel. Coupled with this was the work of Sir George Airy on the correction of compasses which allowed iron ships to go out into the open water. The Admiralty also noted the success of the iron gun vessel *Nemesis.* This boat had been built for the East India Company and successfully operated during the China War. This encouraged the navy to order an iron steam vessel in 1843. Ditchburn & Mare's tender was accepted in April 1843. This was the first iron warship to be ordered by the Royal

HMS Minotaur, *an ironclad built by the Thames Iron Works. The ship was launched in 1863 but not completed until 1868.*

Navy, although she was not the first to be completed. Ditchburn & Mare completed the ship in 1846 and the vessel was named HMS *Trident*. She was classified as a sloop, third class and the armaments were two 10ins pivot guns and two 32-pounder carronades. She had Boulton & Watt oscillating engines of 350nhp which gave her a speed of 9½ knots. Ditchburn & Mare completed another sloop for the Royal Navy in 1847 and she was named *Antelope*. The Admiralty also ordered six iron paddle steamers from two makers. These ships of the 'Jackall' class were completed in 1845 and were the first British naval ships made with iron and propelled by steam machinery. The order for the six ships was divided between the Napier yard in Glasgow and Ditchburn & Mare. Two of the vessels, namely HMS *Lizard* and HMS *Torch* were to be built to Symonds's lines with 145nhp side lever engines. HMS *Jackall* and HMS *Harpy* were built to the same designs but with higher powered engines. The last two, HMS *Bloodhound* and HMS *Myrmidon* were to be designed by the builders with 150nhp engines. Ditchburn & Mare constructed HMS *Torch*, HMS *Harpy* and HMS *Myrmidon* and they were launched in 1845. They proved to be useful ships and had long histories. *Harpy* took part in the Parana River campaign in 1846 and had the distinction of being sunk during the trials for the Zalinski dynamite air gun. The firm of Ditchburn & Mare were also building other iron steam vessels for the government at this time. These however, were not fighting ships but Post Office packets. These included *Princess Alice* (1843) and *Onyx* (1845). This early association between the Admiralty and Ditchburn & Mare with regards to building iron ships would continue at the yard until the early twentieth century. The company also constructed for the Admiralty the only iron sailing ship that entered into service with the British Navy. This was the 470 ton iron brig HMS *Recruit* which was later sold and converted into the merchant ship *Harbinger*. Charles J. Mare operating at the yard on his own built one large iron ship for the navy. This was an iron screw frigate named HMS *Vulcan*. This ship was completed

HMS Sans Pareil, *a 10,470 tons turret ship. She was launched in 1887 and completed in 1891.*

in 1849 and was 220ft long, 1,764 tons with horizontal engines by G.&J. Rennie of London. She was not a successful vessel and was soon converted into a troopship. The *Vulcan* saw service during the Crimean War and it was the opening of these hostilities that prompted more naval orders to be placed with Charles J. Mare. It was soon realised that this war would need a considerable number of gunboats to blockade and attack the Russian coast in the Black Sea and also in the Baltic. Orders for a large number of gunboats were placed with all the major yards on the Thames and elsewhere. These were to be wooden ships and it would be a step back for a yard like Mare's which had been building iron ships. Mare completed twelve gunboats during the period 1854-55. Mare's workers had to re-learn the old methods of building wooden vessels. These vessels had to be completed quickly and this put pressure on several yards. The large number of these boats that had to be built meant that fully seasoned timber for boat building became scarce and expensive. It was believed that Mare lost money on every gunboat that his yard completed and this drove the concern into bankruptcy in 1856 with further gunboats partly built and on the stocks. The reformed Thames Iron Works Company was able to persuade the Admiralty to advance them £9,700 to complete the unfinished gunboats. In January 1856 the government ordered 20 iron mortar vessels at the cost of £2,200 each. Six were to be completed in January, six in February and the remainder in March. There were few yards that had the necessary experience and skills for building iron ships. So it is no wonder that when any new developments were made in iron warships then the Thames Iron Works would be in the forefront of this advance.

Relations between France and Britain took a downward turn after the Crimean War. France began an ambitious program of warship building which resulted in the launch of *Gloire*. This was a vessel which was an ironclad. The hull was wooden but her upper deck was encased in wrought iron

HMS Blenheim, *a 9,150 tons protected cruiser, first class. She was launched by the Thames Iron Works in 1890 and completed in 1894.*

plates which were 4½ins thick and the plates also stretched from stem to stern. The Admiralty's answer was to build two iron clad ships but these would have iron hulls. The ships were named HMS *Warrior* which would be completed by the Thames Iron Works and HMS *Black Prince* which would be built at Napier's yard on the Clyde. *Warrior* was ordered in June 1859. The accepted Thames Iron Works tender was for £31 10s per ton Builders Old Measurement giving the contract total of £190,225. The contract stipulated that the ship was to be launched within eleven months from the date of acceptance which was April 11 1860. The ship was to be ready for completion, except masting, three months later. Payments for this massive contract was to be made in five instalments, the first when the ship was 'in frame'; and the final when 'delivered up complete'. The contract did contain a penalty clause of £50,000. This and the other early ironclads were described as frigates because they only had one deck of guns. These were, in fact, the new breed of battleships. HMS *Warrior* was the first ocean going armoured ship. This contract was the beginning of the love affair between the Thames Iron Works and the building of large capital ships. It also illustrated in this first large contract, the problems that could beset a yard that built these ships. The large beams that made up the structure of the ship were contracted out to the Butterley Iron Company in Derbyshire. There were problems with the delivery and quality of these beams. [42] Any delay might trigger a financial penalty and with later ships built by the Thames Iron Works these delays could come from changes in design from the Admiralty. The whole project was overseen by Captain John Ford who was the managing director of the Thames Iron Works Company. The armour belt over the midships section was 213ft long by 22ft deep and consisted of 15ft x 3ft iron plates weighing four tons each. The plates were tongued and grooved to give support if struck by a shell. This was an expensive method

HMS Theseus, a First Class protected cruiser. The ship was launched in 1892 and completed in 1896.

and was abandoned for later ironclads. The *Warrior* was launched on the 29th December 1860 and completed on 24th October 1861. Her size overall was 420ft x 58ft 4ins x 26ft and her displacement was 9,137 tons. Her screw trunk engine was constructed by Penn of London and worked along a single shaft and propeller. Both HMS *Warrior* and HMS *Black Prince* were re-classified as armoured cruisers in about 1880 when in reserve. HMS *Warrior* was converted to a depot ship in 1902, renamed *Vernon III* in 1904, hulked in 1923 and then used as an oil pipeline pier at Pembroke Dock. She was saved for preservation and underwent a major restoration after which she was taken to Portsmouth Dockyard where she is now a major attraction. The next large ship built for the British Navy by the Thames Iron Works was HMS *Minotaur*. This ship was designed as a 50 gun armoured frigate with full length protection to the battery to avoid unprotected gun positions on the main deck. This type of ship became known as a broadside ironclad. HMS *Minotaur* was laid down in 1861, launched in 1863 and completed in 1865. She was 407ft x 59ft 6ins x 27ft 9ins and of 10,690 tons. However, the ship then spent eighteen months testing experimental armaments and rigs before being commissioned in 1868. She was propelled by a Penn horizontal trunk engine. *Minotaur* was extensively refitted in 1873-75 when she became the first ship in the Royal Navy to carry a searchlight. HMS *Minotaur* was converted to a training ship in 1904 and renamed *Boscawen*, then *Ganges II* in 1908. She was sold out of the navy for breaking up in 1922. In 1866 the Thames Iron Works launched the experimental ship HMS *Waterwitch*. She had been laid down in 1864 and was completed in 1867. She was an armoured gunboat of 1,280 tons. This was an attempt to apply ironclad characteristics to a gunboat. Three ships in this class were built and they were not successful as they were slow and unseaworthy. HMS *Waterwitch* did not have a steam engine but was fitted with hydraulic reaction machinery which was an early form of turbine propulsion designed by J. Ruthven. The engine drove a centrifugal pump which drew in water from openings in the ship's bottom at the front and forced it out under high pressure at the stern giving it a form of jet propulsion. The whole system was reversible and *Waterwitch* was designed as double ended with a rudder and ram shape at both bow and stern. The ship was a complete failure being just about unmanoeuvrable. As this was built to the designs of the Admiralty there could be no criticism of its manufacture by the Thames Iron Works. In the late 1860s and early 1870s the Thames yard built three iron screw corvettes for the navy. They were HMS *Active* (1869), HMS *Volage* (1869) and HMS *Rover* (1874). *Active* was of 3,080 tons and measured 270ft x 42ft x 22ft. In 1875 the Thames Iron Works launched HMS *Superb* which was an ironclad battery. This ship illustrates some of the problems that the Thames Iron Works had to overcome when building ships for the Royal Navy and also for foreign governments. This ship was designed for the Turkish navy as *Hamidieh* but was detained and purchased by Britain because of a war scare with Russia in 1878. It was modified to Admiralty requirements and commissioned into the Royal Navy in 1880. This 9,710 ton ship measured 332ft 4ins x 59ft x 25ft 6ins with a horizontal direct acting engine by Maudslay of London. HMS *Superb* survived into the twentieth century and was sold for breaking up in 1906. HMS *Valiant* which was completed by the Thames Iron Works also demonstrates the problems in building large iron warships. This ship was laid down by Westwood & Baillie of Millwall on the Thames but the firm became bankrupt in 1861. The ship was completed by the Thames Iron Works and was launched in 1863. However, the full completion of this 6,710 ton broadside ironclad did not take place until 1868. Although the yard built two composite gunboats that were launched in 1880 the company had to wait until the mid-1880s to complete a large ship for the Admiralty. This was

HMS Grafton, *the sister ship to* Theseus. *She was launched by the Thames Iron Works in 1892 and completed in 1894.*

The crowd at the launch of HMS Cornwallis, *Thames Iron Works, 17th July 1901.*

HMS *Benbow*, a barbette ship laid down in 1882 and launched in 1885. A barbette took the form of a circular or elongated ring of armour around a rotating gun mount over which a large gun fired. HMS *Benbow* had Maudslay inverted compound steam engines and was 330ft x 68ft 6ins x 27ft 10ins. This 10,600 ton ship was not commissioned until 1888. She served in the Mediterranean from 1888 to 1891 and then as a guard ship at Greenock from 1894 to 1904. She was then kept in reserve until sold for breaking up in 1909.

The continual development of the large capital ships for the British Navy can be seen by the next ship produced for the Admiralty by the Thames Iron Works. This was HMS *Sans Pareil* which was a 10,470 ton turret ship. She was laid down in 1885, launched in 1887 and completed in 1891. This was one of the first battleships to be built with triple expansion engines. These were supplied by Humphrys of London. The completion of this ship was severely delayed by the late delivery of its main armaments. HMS *Sans Pareil* survived until 1907 when she was sold for breaking up. The next

Admiralty orders were for a series of First Class protected cruisers. The first to be laid down in 1888 was HMS *Blenheim* (9,150 tons). This ship was launched in 1890 and completed in 1894 again with triple expansion engines. *Blenheim* served in the Channel Fleet during the period 1894-98 and on the China station during 1901-04. In 1907 she was partially disarmed and converted to a depot ship to be later broken up in 1926. In 1890 the Thames Iron Works laid down two First Class protected cruisers. They were the 7,350 ton HMS *Grafton* and HMS *Theseus*. Both were launched in 1892 with *Grafton* being completed in 1894 and *Theseus* completed in 1896. Although obsolete by 1914 they saw extensive service in the First World War. HMS *Grafton* was sold out of service in 1920 and HMS *Theseus* was sold in 1921.

The launch of HMS Cornwallis at the Thames Iron Works, 17th July 1901.

The Thames Iron Works was also involved in the early development of the destroyer. The works built HMS *Zebra*, first in a batch of destroyers. This ship was laid down in 1894, launched in 1895 and

HMS Cornwallis, *a First Class battleship launched by the Thames Iron Works in 1901 and completed in 1904.*

completed in January 1900. Fully loaded this vessel was 365 tons and measured 200ft x 20ft x 7ft 6ins. She had triple expansion engines that had four cylinders built by Maudslay, Sons & Field of London. These engines were designed to propel the ship to the high speed of 27 knots. The tender for the ship and engines from the Thames Iron Works amounted to £38,598. HMS *Zebra* was not a ship that the Admiralty thought highly of and the Thames Iron Works did not build another destroyer for a decade. *Zebra* spent her career in home waters and was broken up in 1914. [43] In 1898 HMS *Albion* was launched by the Thames Iron works. This 13,150 ton First Class battleship was laid down in 1896 and completed in 1901. The first five ships of this class were designed for the China station to counter the growing naval power of Japan. This class of battleship were the first British battleships to be fitted with water-tube boilers. This ship was a good steamer and on full power trials most of the class achieved 18.5 knots. HMS *Albion* was sold for breaking up in 1919. The management of the Thames Iron Works would have been extremely pleased with the building of this battleship as it seemed to attract further orders for large capital ships from the Admiralty. However, the launch of HMS *Albion* initiated a dreadful accident. A vast crowd had come to watch the launch and many had found their way onto a wooden bridge and pier. When the ship was launched the wave washed many people off these structures into the river. Forty people were drowned and many of these were later buried in a communal grave at East London Cemetery.

In 1901 the works launched two First Class battleships which were HMS *Duncan* and HMS *Cornwallis*. These were two of the six battleships of the 'Duncan' class of over 13,000 tons. These were built in answer to the French and Russian naval building programmes. Four cylinder, triple expansion steam engines were adopted for the ships of this class and it was the first time the Admiralty had used this design. They were good steamers and on trial HMS *Cornwallis* was the best of the class reaching a speed of 19.56 knots. The two Thames ships of this class were laid down in 1899 with

Duncan being completed in 1903 and *Cornwallis* in 1904. HMS *Duncan* was sold for breaking up in 1920 while HMS *Cornwallis* was torpedoed and sunk by U32 east of Malta on 9th January 1917. Another Thames casualty during the First World War was the First Class cruiser HMS *Black Prince*. This ship was laid down in 1903, launched in 1904 and completed in 1906. HMS *Black Prince* was sunk during the Battle of Jutland on 31st May 1916. Another Thames Iron Works ship was also taking part in the action at Jutland. This was HMS *Thunderer*, the last large ship built for the Royal Navy by the Thames Iron Works. *Thunderer* was a massive 22,000 ton 'Orion' Class Super-Dreadnought battleship launched in 1911. The ship had ten 13.5ins guns firing in super-firing turrets. She was over 580ft long and had quadruple propellers driven by Parsons direct acting turbines. She survived the First World War and was decommissioned in 1921 and served as a seagoing training ship for cadets. In 1926 *Thunderer* was sold for breaking up.

The only other Admiralty order in this final period of the history of the Thames Iron Works was for HMS *Nautilus*. This ship was launched in 1910. She was a 'Beagle' class destroyer and was renamed HMS *Grampus* in December 1913. Like several other ships built by the same yard she was involved in the Dardanelles campaign. She was sold for scrapping in 1920.

The launch of HMS Duncan *at the Thames Iron Works, 21st March 1901.*

HMS Duncan *being fitted out at the Victoria Docks of the Thames Iron Works, 1901.*

HMS Duncan, *a 13,745 tons battleship launched at the Thames Iron Works in 1901 and completed in 1903.*

ABOVE LEFT: The fitting of the 9.2ins guns in the forward turret of HMS Black Prince *in 1905.*

ABOVE RIGHT: The port engine of HMS Black Prince.

LEFT: The steam sirens are installed on HMS Black Prince. *The ship was launched in 1904 and completed in 1906.*

Lost in action at Battle of Jutland 1916

HMS Black Prince, an armoured cruiser, First Class built by the Thames Iron Works and sadly lost at the Battle of Jutland, 1916.

HMS Zebra, one of the few destroyers built by the Thames Iron Works. The ship was launched in 1895 and completed in 1900.

HMS Thunderer, *an 'Orion' Class Super-Deadnought, launched at the Thames Iron Works in 1911.*

CHAPTER NINE

SHIPS BUILT BY THE THAMES IRON WORKS FOR FOREIGN NAVIES

The Thames Iron Works built British naval ships over a long period and it was trade that was fraught with problems. Often it took several years to build a large warship and during this time the Admiralty would ask for changes in the construction of the vessel to incorporate new ideas and inventions. If the completion of a vessel was delayed then the yard could be fined by reducing the payment for the ship, this being part of the contract. If any of the sub-contractors were tardy in supplying their parts of the ship to the Thames Iron Works then it would be the shipbuilding yard that would be penalised. The management of the Thames Iron Works accepted this risk and hoped that the production of large capital ships for Britain would encourage foreign governments to place orders for naval vessels. Certainly a large number of orders for ships came to the yard in this way. Many of these ship supplied by the Thames Iron Works to foreign navies and governments were small such as mine layers, gunboats, customs vessels and training ships.

Vitoria, *a centre battery ironclad ship built by the Thames Iron Works in 1865.*

The Greek ironclad ship,
Basileos Georgios, (King
George), *an armour clad
central battery ship built in
1867 by the Thames Iron
Works.*

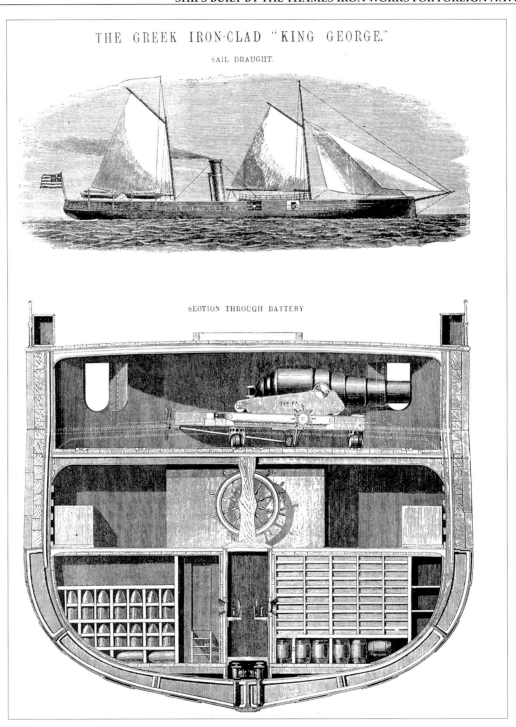

THE GREEK IRON-CLAD "KING GEORGE."

SAIL DRAUGHT.

SECTION THROUGH BATTERY

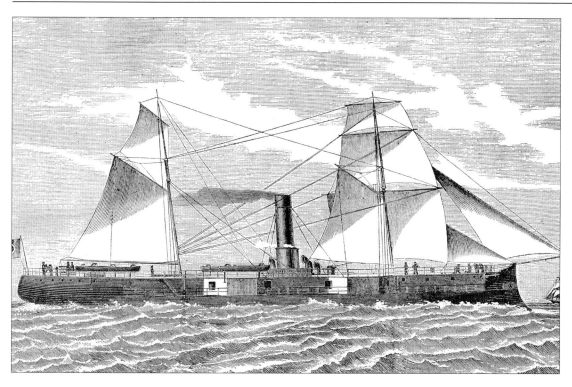

The Turkish ironclad ship Avni Illah *built by the Thames Iron Works for the Turkish Government in 1869.*

After the launch of HMS *Warrior* orders for larger naval ships for foreign navies began to occupy the yard. In the period 1863 – 1865 the Thames Iron works launched seven ships for foreign navies. Four of these ships were gunboats but the other three were much larger contracts. One ship was named *Pervenetz* and was a 3,277 ton coast defence ironclad. This vessel was launched in 1863 and completed in 1864 and was a broadside iron-hulled coast defence ship with a projecting bow. The hull was completely armoured above the water and she was rigged as a three masted schooner. This ship did not take part in any naval actions and was broken up in 1905. In 1864 the yard launched *Mahmudieh* which was built for the Turkish navy. This was a broadside ironclad which had a single telescopic funnel and was rigged as a three-masted barque. This 6,400 ton vessel was 293ft x 55ft 9ins x 25ft 7ins. This ship served as a hulk during the First World War and then scrapped. *Vitoria* was another large naval ship built by Thames during this period. She was an iron hulled centre battery ironclad launched in 1865 for Spain. This was a 7,135 ton ship-rigged vessel with a ram bow. The ship was rebuilt in 1897-98 and after 1900 was used as a training ship.

In the late 1860s and 1870s further orders came to the Thames Iron Works from the Turkish government. This was a market that was laced with problems because of Turkey's chronic finances. The large iron clad *Fatikh,* designed by Sir Edward Reed, was ordered by Turkey from the Thames Iron Works. However, as work progressed on this ship it became apparent that Turkey could not pay for this project. The ship was offered to the British Admiralty and then to the Prussian Navy who purchased her on 6th February 1867. This vessel became the 10,591 ton central battery ironclad *Konig Wilhelm.* She was completed in 1869 and was powered by a horizontal engine working through a single shaft. For some time *Konig Wilhelm* was the largest and most powerful ship in the German Navy and so served as its flagship. In 1895/6 the ship underwent a major rebuild by Blohm & Voss and she was converted to a heavy cruiser. In 1907 she became the school ship of the Naval Academy and was sold off in 1921. Despite all the problems the Thames Iron Works continued to accept further orders for naval ships for Turkey. In the late 1860s the works accepted an order for two ships to be built for the Turkish Navy. The first was launched in 1869 and was *Avni Illah*. She was a small iron-hulled casemate ironclad of 2,362 tons. The ship, rigged as a brigantine, had a ram bow, single funnel and two masts. The ship was lost in 1912 during the Turkish-Italian war. The second ship ordered by Turkey was *Fethi Bulend*, another small casemate ironclad of 2,761 tons which was launched in 1870. Two further naval ships were ordered from the Thames Iron Works by the Turkish government in the mid-1870s. These were *Messudieh*, launched in 1874 and *Memdouhied*, launched in 1875. They were central battery ironclads of 9,120 tons designed by Sir Edward Reed and were based on the design of HMS *Hercules*. *Memdouhied* was renamed *Hamiedieh* while under construction but then purchased by the British Government and renamed HMS *Superb* on 20th February 1878. This was because of a scare that war was imminent with Russia. In 1914 *Messudieh* was moored as a stationary guardship in the Dardanelles off Charnak and there was torpedoed and sunk by the British submarine *B11*. It is amazing to think that during the First World War that there were Thames Iron Works' ships in the navies on opposing sides. Both the navies of the Allies and the navies of the Central Powers had ships that were built by the Thames Iron Works that became casualties of war.

Konig Wilhelm as completed by the Thames Iron Works in 1869 for the Prussian Government

Messoudieh, *a central battery ironclad built in 1874 for the Turkish Government.*

The difficult nature of building naval warships for foreign governments can be illustrated by the ship that the Thames Iron Works would sell to the United States Navy in 1898. This was USS *Topeka*. This vessel was launched in 1881 by Howaldt of Kiel, Germany. She was to be called *Diogenes* and there was a sister ship being built at Kiel at the same time to be called *Socrates* (launched 1880). Both ships were being built as merchant ships for a Portuguese customer. However, tension was building between Peru and Chile and war seemed imminent. The Peruvian government stepped in and purchased the ships in an incomplete state. The ships were taken to the Thames Iron Works for conversion into cruisers for the navy of Peru. However, because of the war an embargo on the sale of these vessels was applied by the British government on these vessels. When the Peruvian government was ready and allowed to take the ships it was realised that they only then required one of the vessels. This vessel was renamed *Lima* and supplied to Peru. However, financing the purchase of this cruiser was a problem so the Thames Iron Works took the other cruiser as payment for the work on the first. It took some time before this ship could be sold. It was thought at one time that the Thames ship had been sold to the Japanese government but the sale fell through and it was not until 1898 that the American government stepped in to purchase the cruiser which was renamed USS *Topeka*. The ship was graded by the Americans as an armed patrol gunboat of 2,372 tons and served the navy until decommissioned in 1929 and then scrapped in 1930. *Lima* was discarded by the Peruvian Navy in 1935.

The Thames Iron Works continued to build several smaller ships for foreign governments but it was not until the mid-1890s that further large contracts were won. These were for the construction of two battleships for the Japanese government. The first battleship was called *Fuji* and was laid down in 1894, launched in 1896 and completed in 1897. This 12,320 ton ship was powered by triple expansion engines with two propellers. She and her sister ship, built by Armstrong Whitworth, were designed by G.C. Mackrow of the Thames Iron Works. *Fuji* took part in the Russo-Japanese War and she fired the last shell at the Battle of Tsushima on 27 May 1905 which sank the Russian ship *Borodino*. *Fuji* was later used as a training ship. She capsized in 1945 and her hulk was scrapped after the war. The second battleship built by the Thames Iron Works for Japan was *Shikishima*. She was laid down in 1897, launched in 1898 and completed in 1900. This 14,850 ton battleship was present at both the Battle of the Yellow Sea and the Battle of Tsushima. She was classed as a coastal defence ship in September 1921 and then disarmed and immobilised under the terms of the Washington Treaty. She later served as a seaman's training ship and was scrapped at Sasebo as late as 1947.

One of the most interesting of the smaller naval ships supplied to governments was the *Immacolata Concezione*. This was supplied to the Pope in 1859 and was described as a Papal yacht of 652 tons. It was, in fact, a screw corvette used primarily for the protection of the fishing trade of the Papal States. The ship had 160hp engines by Seaward & Co. and carried eight 18lb brass cannon. It remained as the flagship of the Papal Navy until the fall of the Pope's temporal power in 1870. The ship was given to a nautical school in 1875 and in 1883 she was sold to a British owner as SS *Gitana* of Glasgow. By 1896 she became French with the name *Loire*. In 1905 she caught fire in the Mediterranean and her gutted hull was lost on the Corsican coast. [44] This was only one example of the many smaller ships supplied to governments around the world which brought fame to the Thames Iron Works.

Vasco da Gama, *an ironclad naval vessel built by the Thames Iron Works in 1878 for the Portuguese Government.*

Gravina and Velasco, *two iron screw cruisers for the Spanish Navy. They were completed by the Thames Iron Works in 1881.*

The Japanese battleship Fuji *built by the Thames Iron Works in 1896.*

The Japanese battleship Shikishima *built by the Thames Iron Works in 1898.*

The problematical USS Topeka, *sold to the United States in 1898 after being converted to a warship by the Thames Iron Works.*

The eight Romanian torpedo vedette boats for the Danube. They are pictured being constructed on the foreshore besides the Thames Iron Works. They were completed in 1906.

The 100ft Romanian torpedo vedette boats receiving their plates in late 1905. Obviously these smaller vessels did not need to be constructed on a slipway.

Vasco da Gama, *a Portuguese ironclad vessel launched by the Thames Iron Works in 1878.*

Principe Dom Carlos, *a 435 ton transport ship for the Portuguese government, launched in 1878.*

CHAPTER TEN

THE THAMES IRON WORKS AND THE PENINSULAR & ORIENTAL COMPANY

One of the largest customers up to 1865 for ships built by the Thames Iron Works was the Peninsular & Oriental Company. This trade started in the mid-1840s and continued until 1865 stretching through the ownership of the yard by Ditchburn & Mare, C.J. Mare and the Thames Iron Works Company. The P&O Company dates from 1837 and was founded by several entrepreneurs but the two main personalities were Arthur Anderson and Brodie McGhie Willcox. [45] It soon started a regular steamer service between London, Spain and Portugal. In 1837 the company won a contract from the British Admiralty to deliver mail to the Iberian Peninsula. Three years later the company acquired a contract to deliver mail to Alexandria in Egypt. The P&O Company now looked to the east for expansion and mail contracts were the basis of its prosperity. Its first ships were chartered but soon the company was ordering ships from several builders on the Thames as London was where the P&O Company had their offices. These ships were early steam vessels which used sails and auxiliary steam engines to provide the motive power.

The first ship built for the P&O by the Thames yard was the iron paddler *Ariel* built when Ditchburn & Mare operated the works. She was 194ft long and she was 709 tons gross. *Ariel* had a pair of oscillating steam engines built by John Penn & Son giving 300ihp which could give her a speed of 9 knots. The ship had been designed for dual use to take passengers and 246 tons of cargo. She was launched in 1846 and completed at a cost of £59,000. *Ariel* was one of the first merchant ships to be built with watertight compartments. She left Malta on 28th May 1848 for Britain via the Italian coast. However, on the 2nd of June she became stranded on the rocks off Mal di Vetro, 13 miles south of Liverno lighthouse. The passengers were rescued by the paddle frigate HMS *Sidon* and later the baggage, valuables and most of the cargo. Salvage of the ship was considered but on 1st July 1848 she broke up during a gale. A second ship for the P&O Company was launched in 1846. This was the 199ft iron paddle steamer originally named *Erin-go-Bragh*. She was to be a passenger liner powered by a pair of steam engines manufactured by Maudslay, Sons & Field. She was also designed to carry 344 tons of cargo. When completed at a cost of £35,000 she was renamed *Erin* and her maiden voyage was from Southampton to the Black Sea. In 1851 she was send out as part of the Calcutta – Penang – Singapore – Hong Kong service and carried P&O's first cargo of Malwa opium from India to China. *Erin* was used during 1852 in carrying troops from Amherst to Moulmein for the Burmese War. She continued in service in the east until 6th June 1857 when she became stranded 34 miles north of Galle, Ceylon when on a voyage from Bombay to China. The passengers, crew and mails were rescued along with 400 out of 1,200 cases of opium that were part of her cargo.

The third ship bought from the yard for the Peninsular & Oriental Company was the *Himalaya*. She was laid down in 1851 at which time the owner of the yard was C.J. Mare. She was to be built as a paddle steamer but was altered while under construction to a screw steamer. This ship had a gross

Himalaya, launched by the Thames Iron Works in 1853 for the Peninsular and Oriental Company. Later it was sold to become a troopship and met her end in 1940 during the Second World War.

tonnage of 3,438 and was 372.9ft x 46.2ft x 43.9ft. *Himalaya* was launched in 1853 by Lady Matheson, wife of P&O Chairman Sir James Matheson. She had a very good claim to be the largest ship in the world and was twice the tonnage of any other P&O ship. She had one shaft and propeller driven by a horizontal direct-acting trunk steam engine by John Penn & Son of Greenwich. *Himalaya* was built at a cost of £132,000. Her maiden voyage took her from Southampton to Alexandria via Malta. In 1854 she was sold for £130,000 to the Government for service as a troopship. The ship was extensively used during the Crimean War. She was fitted with an extra deck and was capable of carrying 1,850 troops. In 1880 she had new engines and boilers installed. In 1894 she was placed in reserve following the closure of the Government troopship service. A year later she was reduced to a hulk by Earle's at Hull and stationed at Devonport as HM *Hulk C60*. In 1910 she was transferred to Chatham and in 1920 she was sold to the Portland & Weymouth Coaling Company Ltd and towed to Portland. For twenty years she was anchored at Portland Harbour but on 4th of July 1940 she was attacked and sunk by German aircraft. *Himalaya* was one of the longest lived ships built at the yard and her story spans continents and several wars. Certainly the ship represents the excellent quality, workmanship and strength that could be turned out by the shipbuilders of the Thames.

As well as needing cargo and passenger steamers the company also needed ships to support these vessels on their long routes. One of these was built by C.J. Mare in 1853. This ship was called *Rajah* and was an auxiliary steam collier. Its gross weight was 600 tons and had a single screw powered by a trunk geared steam engine made by James Watt & Co. of Birmingham. The ship was intended for service east of Suez carrying coal from Labuan in North Borneo to P&O depots throughout the east. She was requisitioned in 1854 for use in the Crimean War. At some time during her stay in the

Crimea she was employed as a floating bakery. After the war she returned to service with P&O but in 1861 *Rajah* was sold to R.D. Sassoon of Hong Kong for use on the China coastal trade. By 1865 the ship was back in London being owned by G. Elliott and in 1875 was sunk in a collision when on a voyage from London to the north east of England. Another collier was built by Mare for the P&O at the same time. This was *Manilla* and had a gross tonnage of 646 with a trunk geared steam engine by Day, Summers & Co. of Southampton. Again this collier was a barque-rigged auxiliary with a screw engine. As with *Rajah* she was requisitioned for service in the Crimean War. In 1858 during the Indian Mutiny she was used for trooping duties on the Indian coast. *Manilla* was sold out of P&O service in 1861. The relationship between Charles Mare and the P&O Company must have been very good as a third ship was launched by Mare for the company. This was *Valetta* which was a 900 ton wooden paddle steamer with oscillating engines by John Penn & Son of Greenwich. She was built of wood as the Admiralty required wooden paddlers only to be used for contract mail services. *Valetta* cost £52,801 10s to build. In 1859 her original engines were found to be too powerful and economic and so they were removed and put in the company's ship *Delta*. New engines by the original engine builder were fitted and found to save 55 per cent on fuel. In 1865 the ship was sold to Henry Bailey and then sold on to the Egyptian Government.

C.J. Mare continued to build ships for the P&O Company throughout the 1850s. The next vessel built for the company was *Candia*, a 2,200 ton iron screw passenger liner. She was launched in 1853 and was completed in 1854 with trunk steam engines by J.&G. Rennie of London. The vessel was built at a cost of £69,200. As with many of these large passenger ships she was requisitioned in 1854 for service in the Crimean War as Transport No 213. She is recorded as carrying P&O's largest lift of troops when

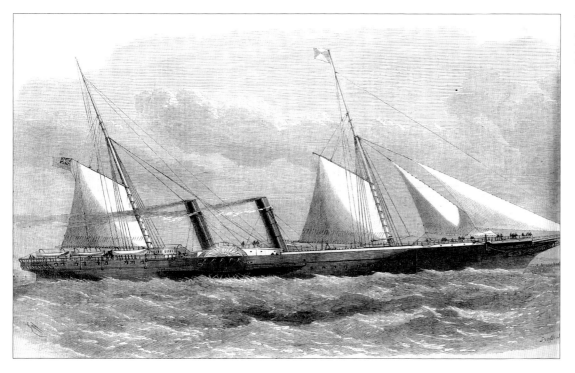

The Peninsular and Oriental's paddle steamer, Delta, *launched at the Thames Iron Works in 1859*

1,159 troops, 32 officers and 6 women were transported from Marseilles to the Crimea. Later she was further lengthened and used on the Suez to Calcutta service. In 1874 she sailed from Southampton as a troopship for the Ashanti War travelling via Plymouth, St. Vincent, Sierra Leone, Cape Coast Castle and then returning to Southampton. In October 1874 she was sold for £12,000 to J. Howden & Co. of Glasgow and later fitted with two cylinder compound engines. In 1877 the ship was sold to Japanese owners and in 1893 was disposed of to Japanese shipbreakers. The last ship completed by C.J. Mare for the P&O was *Pera*, a 2,126 ton passenger liner. This ship was launched incomplete in June 1855 because Mare was on the verge of bankruptcy. It was built at a cost of £69,250 on the principle of 'less power and finer lines'. Her equipment included steam winches, a helmsman's telegraph and Cunningham's patent reefing topsails. The designer of *Pera* was James Ash and the vessel was described as *'the most perfect steamer that ever left the Thames'*. She was occupied on the Southampton/Alexandria service and later the Venice/Bombay service. She was sold out of P&O service by auction in 1880 when William Ross of London bought the vessel for £8,402. In June 1882 she sank after hitting an iceberg 50 miles south-west of Cape Race when on a voyage from Quebec to London.

The first P&O ship built by the new Thames Iron Works Company was the *Nepaul*. It was an iron screw passenger vessel of 796 tons gross. It had a single screw driven by a direct acting inverted steam engine by Humphrys and Tennant of London. It was launched in 1858 and was destined for the Marseilles/Alexandria service. In 1863 it was transferred for service in the Far East. In 1867 the ship was sold to Japanese owners and in 1878 it was reduced to a sailing vessel. The next ship built by the Thames Iron Works was to have much more exotic career. This was the *Delta* which was an iron paddle steamer of 1,618 tons gross. She was launched in 1859 and fitted with oscillating steam engines by John Penn of Greenwich. Her engines had been formerly fitted to *Valetta* but they proved to be too powerful for that vessel. This and her sister ship were to be the last paddle steamers built for the P&O Company and were part of an Admiralty effort to update the paddle system of propulsion. To that end the ship was fitted with the innovation of feathering paddles. She had a short life as a P&O ship and in 1874 was sold to the Japanese Government as a troopship for its Formosa campaign. Later the ship was sold to private owners in Japan and in 1878 it was re-engined by Lobnitz, Coulborn & Co. of Renfrew and converted to a screw steamer. This ship was one of a rare breed for it is notable for being known as one of a few ghost ships. In 1898 it was sold by its Japanese owners to the Centennial Alaska Transportation Co. (C. Nelson & Co.) and renamed *Centennial*. In that year she carried miners and stores to Alaska during the Klondyke Gold Rush. In 1905 it was captured by Japanese forces while attempting to run the blockade of Vladivostok during the Russo-Japanese War but was later released. On 24th of February 1906 it sailed from Muroran for San Francisco but never arrived. Seven years later a Russian expedition found it abandoned and locked in the ice north of Sakhalin.

The next ship built by the Thames Iron Works was of a much more modern aspect. This was the single screw passenger liner *Mooltan* which was launched in 1860. It had a 2,257 gross tonnage and was powered by tandem compound steam engines constructed by Humphrys, Tennant & Co of Deptford. The ship could cater for 112 First Class passengers and 37 Second Class. The ship was constructed for the Southampton/Alexandria and Calcutta/Suez services. This was the first of the company's ships to be fitted with compound engines, and these halved fuel consumption but were unreliable and broke down frequently. However, the vessel was known for her comfort with magnificent fittings including a hydraulic ice-making machine for the passengers. In 1880 the ship was sold to J. Ellis & Co. of Liverpool then sold in 1884 to J. Pedley of London. The ship was renamed *Eleanor Margaret* and reduced to a sailing ship. On 18th of June 1891 she sailed from Newcastle upon Tyne for Valparaiso and disappeared without trace in the North Atlantic.

The close link between the P&O Company and the Thames Iron Works continued during the early 1860s. In 1863 Thames launched the *Golconda* for the company. This was a single screw passenger steamer of 1,909 tons gross. The ship was 314.5ft long and had tandem compound direct-acting steam engines built by Humphrys, Tennant & Dykes of Deptford. The vessel was destined for the Suez/Bombay service and survived as a P&O ship until 1881 when it was sold for £5,311 to B. Mohamed Habdue Rayman for demolition at Bombay. In 1864 the Thames Iron Works launched the *Nyanza* for the P&O Company. This was a paddle steamer of 2,082 tons gross with oscillating steam engines constructed by J.&G. Rennie of London. This vessel was built for the Southampton/Alexandria service but only saw service for a short time as the vessel was sold in 1873 for £26,000 to the Union Steam Ship Company of Southampton. Later she became the private yacht of the Sultan of Zanzibar, She was sold in 1904 to Indian shipbreakers at Bombay.

The final order to the yard from the P&O Company was to build the *Tanjore*. She was launched in 1865 by Miss Ford, the niece of Captain Ford who was the managing director of the Thames Iron Works. The ship was of 1,971 tons gross with a single screw driven by tandem compound engines manufactured by Ravenhill, Salkeld & Co. Her passenger capacity was 118 First Class and 30 Second Class with room for 56,550 cubic feet of cargo. *Tanjore* was built for the Southampton/Alexandria service and later she was used on other Eastern services. In 1875 she was being used on the Calcutta to London service. She was sold in 1888 for £6,794 to Baladina & Co. of Bombay and in 1894 she was sold to shipbreakers at Bombay. After the construction of *Tanjore* the orders from the P&O to the Thames Iron Works dried up. The management of the works believed that more Scottish board members had been recruited by the P&O Company and so orders were then being directed to the Clyde rather than the Thames. It was more likely a factor of costs for the Scottish builders were far closer to the producers of iron and steel than the Thames Iron Works and so overall raw material costs could be much lower. This is clearly seen in the setting up of the shipbuilding activities of the neighbouring Millwall Ironworks which was founded in 1863. That company were making efforts at the outset to purchase an ironworks in South Wales and so keep their costs of raw materials as low as possible. [46]

HMS Sans Pareil, *a 10,470 tons turret ship photographed on a slip at the Thames Iron Works. The hull of the vessel seems to have been completed and she stands ready for the launch which took place in 1887.*

CHAPTER ELEVEN

SOME OTHER NOTABLE COMMERCIAL SHIPS BUILT BY THE THAMES IRON WORKS

In these final chapters I will deal with some other interesting ships built by the Thames Iron Works. I use the Thames Iron Works term loosely as I will be describing ships built at the Orchard and Bow Creek shipyards through all the different owning groups such as Ditchburn & Mare, Charles J. Mare and the various Thames Iron Works companies. As we have seen some large ships were built at these yards for the P&O Company but the Thames yard also built many large ships for the General Screw Steam Shipping Company (GSSSCo.). The yard built at least twenty-four ships for this company with the majority being built during the sole ownership of the yard by C.J. Mare. The GSSSCo. had its roots in a company called The London, Rotterdam & Harlingen Steam Schooner Shipping Company owned by James Laming, William Margetson and John Margetson of Mark Lane, London. Laming had operated sailing ships for about thirty years between England and the Netherlands. His new company would be operating steam ships and it started by ordering several vessels from the yard of Ditchburn & Mare which during the building of these ships became C.J. Mare alone. These ships included the *City of London, City of Rotterdam, Sir John Peel* and *Lord John Russell.* These were fairly small steam ships of around 157 to 206 tons with Maudslay or Penn engines. The vessels were schooner rigged as befitting the title of the company.

This must have been a successful venture for soon other steamships were ordered and the title of the company was changed to the General Screw Steam Shipping Company. In 1849 this company began a service from Liverpool to Gibraltar, Malta and Constantinople using its new iron screw steamer the 531 ton *Bosphorus* which had been launched in that year by C.J. Mare. This was an auxiliary iron screw steamer with twin cylinder diagonal engines by Maudslay, Sons & Field. Two other similar sized ships *Hellespont* and *Propontis* joined *Bosphorus* on this service. Both of these ships were launched by C.J. Mare in 1849. These early screw steamers used their engines as auxiliary motive power to their main sailing capabilities. Soon the GSSSCo. were gaining more mail contracts. One was for a route between Plymouth and Cape Town which was worth £30,000 a year. The *Bosphorus* started this service in December 1850 and sailed to Cape Town in no less than forty days which was five days within the stipulated time in the contract. More orders for ships came to C.J. Mare's yard from this company, maybe because it was widely known that Mare had invested heavily in the GSSSCo.

The shipping company must have met with great success for soon several iron steamers were being ordered from C.J. Mare These were *Queen of the South* (1851, 1,034 tons), *Lady Jocelyn* (1851, 1,650 tons), *Indiana* (1852, 1,179 tons), *Calcutta* (1852, 1,664 tons), *Mauritius* (1852, 1,379 tons) and *Hydaspes* (1852, 1,900 tons). These orders were placed because the GSSSCo. had secured a further mail contract. This was to provide a mail service between England and Madras and Calcutta travelling via Cape St. Vincent, Ascension Island, St. Helena, Cape Town, Mauritius and Ceylon. The company also started a mail service between Cape Town and Durban using the small steam ship *Sir Robert Peel* (launched at Mare's yard, 1846). In 1853 the GSSSCo. began a mail service to Australia using their new ship built by C.J. Mare, *Argo* (1853, 1,653 tons). *Argo* left Southampton on 8th May 1853 and reached Melbourne in 64 days. She returned via Cape Horn and became famous as the first steamer to circumnavigate the world. However, there were problems developing when the company's service to India was withdrawn after poor results. The Australian service was also withdrawn after securing a short term mail contract. The company had high hopes of their Australian service and several new ships had been ordered from C.J. Mare, they were *Golden Fleece* (1853, 2,091 tons), *Jason* (1853, 1,985 tons), *Croesus* (1853, 1,897 tons) and *Prince* (1854, 2,131 tons). At this time C.J. Mare also built several smaller ships for the GSSSCo. Some of these newer large ships did make voyages to Australia.

In March 1854 *Indiana* (launched by Mare, 1852, 1,179 tons) started a new service for the company from Le Harvre and Southampton to New York. It was intended that *Mauritius* would also sail on this route. In July 1854 the company agreed to operate a monthly service between Mauritius and Ceylon for £10,000 a year. However, the plans the company had to operate new services came to a complete halt when their whole fleet was requisitioned by the British Government as troopships for the Crimean War in 1854-55. Their ships were to give great service in the Baltic and Black Sea during the war. The chartering of the fleet allowed the company a period to consider their commercial activities. The General Screw Steam Shipping Company before the war was making large losses on their mail contracts but what could they do after the war? James Laming was now only a director and the chairman of the company was a Mr Ellis. Laming believed that the way ahead was that after the end of the war the company should concentrate on their Indian services. He suggested that in the early history of the company profits were made because of the use of wind and auxiliary steam power. When the company switched to ordering ships with mainly steam power it was then the financial problems began. Laming as the founder of the company wanted the firm to continue. [47] However, there were to be problems with the returning ships which had been worked hard during the period of the war. Many were in a bad state and three had been lost, *Prince* had been destroyed during a storm in 1854, *Mauritius* was badly damaged due to a fire when she was in dry dock in Southampton in February 1855 and *Croesus* was destroyed by fire in the April of the same year. Laming's ideas were rejected and it was decided that the company would cut its losses and sell all the ships. It was not only the building of the Crimean gunboats at his yard that propelled C.J. Mare into bankruptcy. He had invested heavily in the General Screw Steam Shipping Company and the Crimean war had brought matters to a head with the folding of the company and associated losses. It is interesting to note that in Laming's pamphlet of 1855 that outlines his ideas for the company he mentions Captain Ford as an ex-superintendent of the company's ships. It was to be that Captain Ford that steered Mare's yard into the fame and successes of the 1860s.

As well as constructing some large commercial steamers the Thames Iron Works built many interesting smaller ships. Two of these smaller steam ships were subcontracted to the company by James Watt & Co. This company had received the order for these ships from an agency, Anthony Gibbs & Son. The Soho works built the engines and subcontracted the hulls to the Thames Iron Works. James Watt & Co. had built several engines for Thames ships. These 115 ton cargo/passenger gunboats were ordered by the Peruvian Government for service on Lake Titicaca. They were built in kit form with no piece greater than 3½cwt so that the pieces could be transported on mule from the coast to be put together on the shore of the lake. The hulls were ready by 1862 and on 15th October the ship *Mayola* left London with the two ships in pieces and eight engineers. The ships

Dolphin, *an 86 ton tender for South Africa. The ship was completed by the Thames Iron Works in 1882.*

were to be named *Yavari* and *Yapura*. The ship docked at the port of Arica and the Peruvian Navy had the herculean task of transporting 2,766 pieces and two crankshafts to Lake Titicaca, 12,500ft above sea level. Great problems were encountered with getting the parts to the lake and *Yavari* was only launched in 1870. The sister ship, *Yapura* was launched in 1873. In 1924 *Yavari's* steam engines were replaced by a Swedish Bolinder four cylinder hot-bulb semi diesel engine. *Yavari* was disused for many years but has now been restored and is open to the public daily. In 1976 *Yapura* was converted into a hospital ship and renamed BAP *Puno* and is still moored on the lake side.

I finish my review of ships built by the Thames Iron Works with an interesting experimental paddle steamer launched in 1874. This was the 295ft 6ins long *Castalia* built for the English Channel Steamship Company. She was twin hulled with the paddles between the two hulls. She was propelled by two diagonal compound steam engines by J.&A. Blyth of London. The vessel could carry 700 passengers and the designer thought that the ship would be more stable and produce less seasickness for the passengers. The ship was designed with bows forward and astern in order to avoid the need to turn around at Calais. *Castalia* and her sister ship, which was built in the North East of England were not a success. In 1881 *Castalia* was put up for sale and purchased for £5,500 by the Metropolitan Asylums Board. She was converted to a hospital ship for 150 patients and served in this capacity until 1904. In December of that year she was sold for £1,120 and broken up.

HMS Albion, *A 13,150 tons battleship first class built by the Thames Iron Works. The vessel was launched in 1898 and completed in 1901.*

An artists' impression of the tragic scene following the launch of HMS Albion.

CHAPTER TWELVE
THE ALBION DISASTER

The Thames Iron Works and the ships it built produced some notable stories. However, the saddest point in the history of the company must have been the disaster that took place with the launching of HMS *Albion* in 1898. The ship was a 390ft long First Class battleship with a load weight of 13,150 tons. The keel of the ship was laid down in 1896 and the launching of the hull took place on 21st June 1898. Huge crowds turned out to view the launch. The crowds were attracted to the event as the shipyard was honoured with the presence of the Duke and Duchess of York. They were a popular couple. He was the heir apparent and had served in the Royal Navy before the death of his elder brother. The Duchess of York had the honour of naming and launching the ship.

The Thames Iron Works had printed 20,000 tickets for the launch. Prepared seating accommodated about 8,000, the remaining spectators would watch from various points around the shipyard. Launching ships could be a dangerous proposition. Fifteen years earlier no less than a hundred lives had been lost with the launching of the *Daphne* on the Clyde. Many of the spectators that came to view the *Albion* launch had ventured into unsafe areas to watch the launch. This included a wooden bridge over a creek. This bridge was used by small numbers of workmen and was not designed for a huge crowd. The area appears to have been marked with some danger signs but was guarded by few policemen who would not have known that this area would be inundated by water as this huge ship hit the water. As the ship entered the water a backwash overtook the bridge. On the bridge were between one to two hundred people mainly dock workers and their families. Most of the people at the launch did not see this dreadful event unfold as their eyes were on the ship as it came to rest in the water. Soon people were fighting for their lives in the dark, muddy waters. Cries were drowned out by the general hullabaloo of the launch. However, when the predicament of the crowd in the water was spotted there were many acts of heroism as people jumped into the water to save lives. As well as the police several civilians were prominent in the rescues. However, a number of bodies were recovered and although estimates vary it is thought thirty eight people drowned at the *Albion* launch. The Royal Humane Society later awarded twenty four bronze medals in recognition of the life-saving exploits of some of the bystanders. Amongst the spectators was Robert Paul who was an early filmmaker. He not only caught the launch on camera but also some of the aftermath of the disaster. The film did cause controversy as some felt that Paul should be helping in rescue attempts rather than continue to film.

Arnold Hills was overcome with grief at the tragedy. He visited the homes of the bereaved as, *'In some senses I represented the Company at whose doors the responsibility of this great accident lay …'*. Few seemed to blame the company and Hills was later to record that *'I pray to God that so long as he may spare me I may be enabled to do something for the well-being and happiness of Canning Town'*. Within twenty four hours of the accident Hills had purchased a large plot in East London Cemetery. The *Albion* was launched on a Tuesday and the dead were buried on the following Saturday, Monday and Tuesday. Many were buried in the communal grave with others being buried in their own graves at East London Cemetery and at other locations.

London & South Coast Motor Service Ltd operated a fleet of eight Thames Ironworks' char-à-bancs which, it is recorded, amassed 168,200 miles between them. The location is unclear but the feeling is that the tour is about to set off for a day's outing.

NATIONAL MOTOR MUSEUM

One of John Cann's London & South Coast Motor Service Ltd. char-à-bancs outside the firm's Folkestone, Kent, offices. The date would be circa 1906-1907.

NATIONAL MOTOR MUSEUM

CHAPTER THIRTEEN

MOTOR VEHICLES BUILT BY THE THAMES IRON WORKS

by Malcolm Bobbit

Similarly to a number of heavy engineering and shipbuilding, companies, Thames Iron Works addressed the coming of the motor age by diversifying briefly into the production of steam vehicles before concentrating on motor cars and commercial vehicles. The arrival of the internal combustion engine had signalled a major shift in road transport, and whilst a large number of firms remained committed to steam, it was the petrol, and later diesel, engine that influenced future technology.

Before the advent of the motor vehicle, steam had been the principal means of providing power, its use for road transport having supplanted the stagecoach and other horse-drawn carriages, all of which were often slow and uncomfortable. Though the first steam vehicle to run under its own power had been constructed in France in 1769 by Nicolas-Joseph Cugnot, it was not until the middle of the following century that steam wagons and coaches came into prominence, and even then were frequently unreliable. When applied to industry and agriculture, steam traction engines proved to be quite efficient, but then steam road transport received a fillip when, in 1861, an act of parliament reduced the tolls that were payable to use Britain's roads. A setback came four years later in 1865 when another act of parliament, the Road Locomotive Act, limited the speeds of all mechanically propelled vehicles to 4mph in rural areas and 2mph in towns and cities, and in addition required a man holding a red flag to walk 60 yards in front of the machine.

When the so-called red-flag act was repealed on 14th November 1896 it gave impetus to the advancement of the internal combustion engine. Steam vehicles, both cars and commercial types, nevertheless continued to be developed, some seriously rivalling petrol vehicles in terms of power and performance. For example, in 1901 the French engineer Léon Serpollet took the world record for the 'flying kilometre' and the following year held the land speed record with a speed of 75.06mph. Steam wagons were at this time popular since they were preferred to petrol versions owing to their expediency when carrying heavy loads. They finally lost favour in the 1920s and 1930s when vehicles were taxed according to their unladen weights, and thus were quickly displaced by petrol engined types which were becoming much more efficient.

Some well-established engineering companies built steam vehicles to include Thornycroft of Chiswick in West London; Knight of Farnham in Surrey; Foden of Elworth in Cheshire, Atkinson in Lancashire and Sentinel of Glasgow, all progressing to petrol and diesel power and becoming familiar sights on Britain's highways. A number of steam vehicle manufacturers were located in London, many situated near or alongside the River Thames: Walter Hancock had his engineering business at Stratford and was famous for his steam coaches plying in London and elsewhere while Frank Hills built steam buses at his premises at Deptford. Sir Alfred Yarrow, the torpedo manufacturer, designed a four-wheeled steam carriage in the mid-1800s and had it constructed by T.W. Cowan of Greenwich (he was previously employed at the Kent Ironworks), this being displayed at the Great London

Exposition at South Kensington in 1862.

Despite Thames Iron Works' remarkable record of shipbuilding, by the turn of the century the firm was seeking to diversify its activities. The construction of large ships on the River Thames was in decline, and merging with the marine engineering business of John Penn and Sons in 1898 offered Thames Iron Works a suitable solution. John Penn established his business in 1799 and it grew to become one of the largest and most important engineering works in London. His son, also John, joined the business in the early 1830s and was revered for his design of an oscillating engine for use in paddle steamers, while his patented trunk engine was employed on naval screw-propelled vessels. The esteem in which the company was held led to it becoming the principal engine supplier to the Royal Navy during the transition from sail to steam.

The merger between John Penn and Sons and Thames Iron Works allowed the latter to undertake the construction of steam road wagons at the former's site at Greenwich. The aforementioned Frank Hills was not only involved in the merger, but also his son Arnold was instrumental in the manufacture of steam vehicles for a short time before turning his attention to motor vehicles. Steam wagons were built by Thames Iron Works using the Thames name from 1902, the most significant being a five-ton wagon designed by Hills which that year made its debut test run from Blackheath Hill to Bromley, when it used 79 gallons of water, three quarters of coke and recorded a speed of 5mph.

Arnold Hills was quick to recognise that steam would lose out to the motor age for road transport, and therefore Thames looked to develop a range of petrol-engined vehicles. Though it is mostly recorded that Thames Iron Works commenced the production of motor vehicles in 1906, newspapers and motoring publications were announcing the company's plans the preceding year. Thames constructed its first omnibus chassis in 1905, which it exhibited at that year's Olympia exhibition alongside a petrol delivery van and a steam wagon. Thames was also involved in the design and manufacture of its own internal combustion engines, these including two six-cylinder types, one of 45hp, the other 60hp, that were produced in 1906 and intended to propel the firm's char-à-bancs. Four-cylinder engines of 24/30hp were also being produced which were suitable for smaller commercial vehicles and motor cars.

The char-à-bancs proved to be popular with operators, one in particular being John Cann of Folkestone in Kent who replaced his fleet of MMC vehicles with those built by Thames. Cann was impressed by the char-à-banc's design, recording that the removable, covered coupé section at the rear afforded welcome protection for passengers in wet or windy weather. John Cann changed the name of his company to London & South Coast Motor Service Ltd and it is documented that by 1908 he was operating no fewer than eight Thames Iron Works' char-à-bancs, which between them had clocked up a total of 168,200 miles.

The following year, 1907, a 10-15cwt commercial chassis was designed with a 10/12hp engine. One of these chassis was fitted with a novel body in the shape of a tyre section to the order of Palmer Tyres, then a foremost tyre manufacturer, this probably being one of the first vehicles of its type to be designed specifically as a marketing tool. Having an overall weight of 45cwts it competed in the Commercial Vehicle Trials that were overseen by the RAC that November, and featuring a heavy axle it was capable of carrying a one ton payload. The vehicle's entry into the trials was not to test the ability of the Thames engine and chassis, but instead to gauge the efficiency of the four 5-inch section Palmer tyres that were fitted to the machine.

By 1908 the Thames Iron Works' range of commercial vehicles had grown to include a three-

BELOW : The marketing of Thames Iron Works' vehicles was undertaken by Walter Thomas Clifford-Earp Ltd, this photograph showing Clifford-Earp at the wheel of the 60hp Thames racing car which broke speed records at Brooklands in 1907. Alongside is his brother Arthur, acting as his riding mechanic.

NATIONAL MOTOR MUSEUM

ton lorry and a 15hp taxicab. The latter complied with Scotland Yard regulations known as the Conditions of Fitness, thus with its ground clearance and tight turning circle it was suitable for working on London's streets. Though built by Thames Iron Works, the cabs were put on the market by W.T. Clifford-Earp Ltd of 74 Mortimer Street, Regent Street, London W, the name being familiar to Napier historians. In describing the cab, *Commercial Motor* in April 1908 noted that both the exterior and interior coachwork was *'all the more elaborate than otherwise seen on motor cabs, and therefore well-suited to private service or 'betterclass' hiring work.'*

Former Napier employee C.K. Edwards was responsible for designing Thames Iron Works' vehicles, hence similarities exist between the two marques. The aforementioned Walter Thomas Clifford-Earp (his name varies from time to time with and without the hyphen) was also much involved with Napier: he commenced his career with the company as a factory test driver working in the drawing office before Napier relocated from Lambeth to Acton in West London in 1903. Napier, which had built its first car in 1900, enjoyed the highest reputation for its marine and aero engine design, and its motor cars were in a league occupied by Daimler and Rolls-Royce. As an aside, Napier had plans to buy the failing Bentley company in 1930-1931, only for the latter to be snatched from Napier's hands by Rolls-Royce in court under a sealed bid arrangement. Clifford-Earp, and his brother Arthur who was often his riding mechanic in motor sport events, was frequently seen at the helm of a Napier in speed trials.

A 1907 advertisement for the Thames 50/60hp revealed a motor carriage of as high quality engineering one might expect from a notable shipbuilder. The 50hp model was capable of a claimed 50mph while the 60hp could achieve a top speed of 60mph. Both cars had a seating capacity of seven

This decorative full-page advertisement was placed in the October 29th 1910 edition of The Autocar. *It cleverly depicts Thames Iron Works' multiple facets to include shipbuilding and marine engineering along with motor production. Note the reference to the 60hp record breaking activities at Brooklands.*

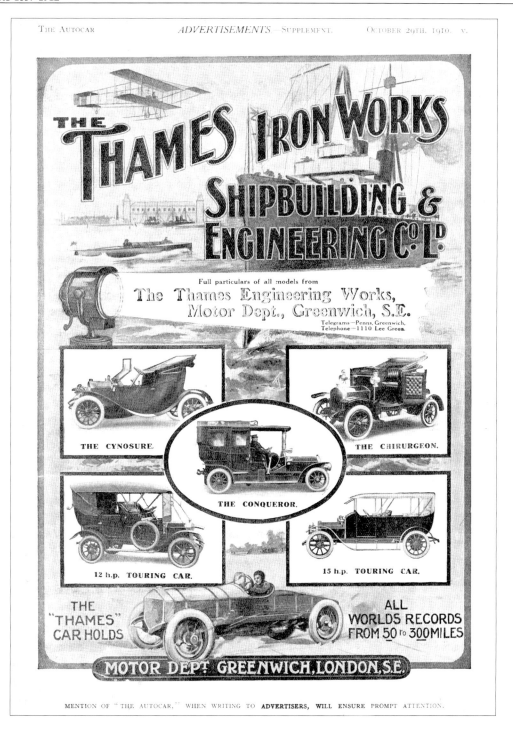

Thames' promoted its 15hp Landaulette as being 'A Gentleman's Carriage'. Clearly the car is of the highest quality, the 'gentleman' being protected from the elements, though in fine weather the hood could be lowered. The chauffeur had only limited protection from the fold-away cover.

RICHARD ROBERTS ARCHIVE

people, the lower-powered version commanding a chassis price of £875 and £950 complete with body, while the 60hp was priced at £950 and £1,050 respectively. W.T. Clifford-Earp Ltd proudly claimed the vehicle having completed the by now seemingly mandatory London to Edinburgh non-stop test (as instigated by the likes of Rolls-Royce, Daimler and Napier), and the acutely arduous London to Dundee run taken in top gear.

Walter Thomas Clifford-Earp was a highly respected pioneer motorist and racing driver. He competed against the leading names in motor sport during its formative years, such as S.F. (Selwyn) Edge of Napier, Charles Jarrott and Lt. Col. Mark J. Mayhew. In addition to driving for Napier, Clifford-Earp competed at Brooklands in 1907 in an Iris for which he was awarded the Marcel Renault Memorial Trophy. Clifford-Earp Ltd is recorded as being the agent for Iris as well as for Thames, and it comes as no surprise that Thames Iron Works and Iris occupied adjacent stands (77, Thames Iron Works; 78, Iris) at the 1909 London Olympia Motor Show.

It was with Clifford-Earp's influence and encouragement that Thames Iron Works took prominence at Brooklands in 1907 by spectacularly breaking a series of speed records. The Brooklands Automobile Racing Club (BARC) had historically held 24-hour records, but decided to recognise additional records over six class categories based on horsepower rating, i.e. 16, 21, 26, 40, 60 and 90. It was anticipated that S.F. Edge would take all the classes in his Napiers, but that changed when Clifford-Earp arrived on the scene on December 10th with his six-cylinder, 9.65 litre 60hp Thames racing car. Not only did the Thames monster set world records for the 50 miles and 150 miles, it also set the

MOTOR CARRIAGES.

RELIABLE. ECONOMICAL.

45 H.P. 6 CYL.
24 H.P. 4 CYL.
12 H.P. 2 CYL.
8 H.P. 1 CYL.

ASK FOR CATALOGUE.

THE THAMES IRONWORKS
SHIPBUILDING & ENGINEERING CO., LTD.,

MOTOR DEPARTMENT,
GREENWICH, S.E.

1 and 2 hours, the speeds recorded as 76.58, 75.95, 76.26 and 75.95mph respectively. Two years later in November 1909, Charles M. Smith in possibly the same car swept away the records by storming 300 miles in excess of 87mph. Believing he could better his own performance, he drove a further 50 miles, the reward being an average speed of 91.32mph. Charles Smith campaigned a 16.9hp Thames at Brooklands in a private competition event in June 1911, taking the award for the best lap at a speed of 61.41mph. Later that year a driver by the name of McNeil entered what appears to be the same Thames 16.9hp at Brooklands, but without winning any awards. The 60hp Thames, which had achieved so much with Charles Smith at the wheel in 1909, was back in action at Brooklands in July 1913 when driven by one Allen, but this time the honours went to Sunbeam, and a DFP driven by Walter Owen Bentley a little under a decade before the latter established Bentley Motors. By the time the 1913 event was held, Thames cars were no more, the company having fallen into receivership.

During its relatively short career, Thames Iron Works produced a number of interesting vehicles ranging from motor vans, lorries, char-à-bancs, omnibuses and motor carriages which also became known as touring cars. What surely looks to be one of Thames Iron Works' earliest machines is an omnibus built in the style reminiscent of a traditional stage coach, but propelled by an internal

ABOVE : Thames' 1909 range of cars is announced in this advertisement which appeared in the Olympia Motor Show catalogue. It depicts the 24hp four-cylinder model which became known as the Champion. All of the firm's models were noted for their engineering quality and bespoke coachwork.

RICHARD ROBERTS ARCHIVE

During 1909 Thames Iron Works produced a beautifully presented colour catalogue, in this instance showing the single-cylinder 8hp Cynosure two-seater. It was designed to have frictionless transmission but when the car went into production it had a conventional gearbox.
NATIONAL MOTOR MUSEUM

From the same 1909 colour catalogue is this rendering of the Chirurgeon two-cylinder Doctor's Coupé. Like the Cynosure, this car was finely engineered but was overly expensive, hence it attracted few customers.
NATIONAL MOTOR MUSEUM

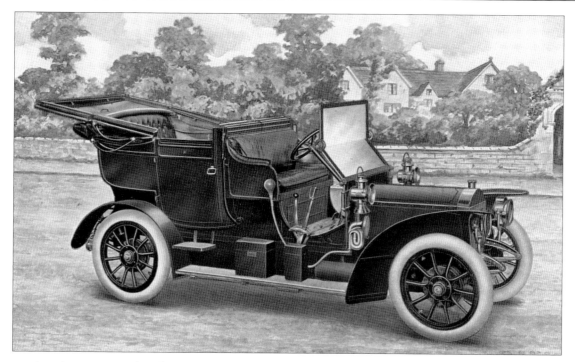

The 24hp touring car, known as the Champion, was the product of exquisite engineering. It was also exceptionally well-appointed and is depicted here in its open position. The hood could be easily raised when required.

NATIONAL MOTOR MUSEUM

combustion engine rather than being horse drawn. A truly magnificent vehicle, it accommodated up to six passengers inside and, according to a period photograph, seated something like sixteen atop the roof on purposely designed cushioned seats. Interestingly, the insignia on the radiator grille is in the form of a large letter 'T', which is not dissimilar to that used by Thornycroft for its lorries post-Second World War. Instead of being constructed in the early 1900s, or earlier, as its design suggests, it was built as late as 1913. In 1911, Thames Iron Works had established a subsidiary company, Motor Coaches Ltd of 29-31 Piccadilly, the address being shared by the Piccadilly Hotel. The idea was to build a number of vehicles modelled closely on the lines of old road coaches, and that a fleet of vehicles would have soon been in service in and around London for the conveyance of pleasure parties. This was a very early attempt at providing what would today would be termed as a 'retro' vehicle. The bodywork was constructed by the esteemed coachbuilder Thrupp & Maberly, which was highly respected for its coachwork for Rolls-Royce and other prestige marques. Thrupp & Maberly later became part of Rootes, the manufacturer of Humber, Hillman, Singer, Sunbeam and Sunbeam-Talbot as well as Commer and Karrier commercials. An example of the coach, most probably the sole vehicle that was constructed, was discovered in Harold Goodey's scrap yard at Twyford in Berkshire where it had been preserved rather than left to rot and then broken up. For some time it was exhibited at the National Motor Museum at Beaulieu in the New Forest, but it now resides in The Hague at the Louwman Museum which specialises in historic vehicles. Though Thames Iron Works went into receivership in 1911, Motor Coaches Ltd survived another two years.

For 1909, Thames announced a range of cars that commenced with a demure single-cylinder 8hp Victoria with friction 'variable gear' transmission and worm-driven rear axle. This was the Cynosure (a name associated with the cosmos) which was definitely in the light car class. Certainly

a curvaceous machine, while it appeared of light weight – it weighed 10cwt without its body – it was far from being anything like flimsy. Beautifully designed and constructed, it benefitted from attention to detail and quality engineering. It is likely that difficulties were experienced during the car's development regarding the friction transmission since the production model was fitted with a conventional gearbox. At £240 the Cynosure was outlandishly expensive when its competitors were commanding in the region of £180 or less, which is why few orders were forthcoming, thus summoning the price to be reduced to £160. Even at the lower price the car failed to attract customers.

A very different car was the two-cylinder Chirurgeon that was built in the style of the then popular two-seater doctor's coupé. The difficult to pronounce name did little to engender sales, but of course anyone with a medical background would have known this to be an archaic term for a surgeon. Again quality engineering was to the fore, but at £235 it was outpriced by its competitors. Thames fared little better with its 15hp Landaulette which it advertised as being 'A Gentleman's Carriage', but strangely the advertisements did not indicate a price, which would have been in the region of £350. There were two top of the range Thames cars: one was the 24hp, four-cylinder Champion priced at £450, its quality rivalling that of the finest bespoke touring cars then available; the other was the 50hp, 7,774cc six-cylinder Conqueror, which commanding £675 was a truly magnificent limousine fit for aristocracy and designed to be chauffeur driven. Though the catalogue clearly states the car being named as the Conqueror, it was often referred to as 'The Emperor', possibly because this seemed a more appropriate appellation.

To accompany the Thames range of cars that were exhibited at the London Olympia Motor Show in November 1909, an elaborate brochure in fine colour was produced, the renderings highlighting

Under its subsidiary Motor Coaches Ltd., Thames Iron Works continued building omnibuses until 1913. This is probably the sole vehicle built and resembles a stage coach; it was designed to convey pleasure parties around London. It is now at the Louwman Museum in The Hague.

NATIONAL MOTOR MUSEUM

the vehicles' superior design and quality engineering. The firm's publicity took an upward turn with full-page advertisements being taken in *The Autocar* and *The Motor* and their like to show the complete model range in an artistic layout, and making much of the company's success at Brooklands. An anomaly with Thames Iron Works' advertising is that during 1911 some of the copy carries the Greenwich address (which superseded that of Clifford-Earp's Mortimer Street), while in other instances the Piccadilly address is shown. Thames Iron Works' publicity department keenly associated its motor cars with its shipbuilding prowess and in particular HMS *Thunderer*; and just in case the message needed any explanation, it was said of the Thames car that *'It is built on sound engineering principles by the builders of Briton's largest Battleships'*

Despite Thames' imaginative publicity and the firm's recognition for quality engineering, its cars failed to attract orders in any meaningful numbers. The 1909 range of cars continued through to the end of 1911, by which time the company had fallen victim to the receiver.

Few Thames Iron Works' vehicles are known to have survived to mark the existence of a very British motor car.

APPENDIX 1
THE PRODUCTS OF THE THAMES IRON WORKS

(A) Ships Built by The Thames Iron Works

This list includes the ships built in 1838 at Dudman's Dock in Deptford, London. During that year a fire forced the company to move to the Orchard House Shipyard. The information for this list comes from many sources which are listed in the references. The main sources are the Thames Iron Works Historical Catalogue which was published in 1911 which was extensively used in the ship lists published by Arnold. I have managed to find a few more ships that are not listed in these two works for the main period of the Thames Iron Works and have also added much detail and histories of the vessels. Records inherited by the Thames Iron Works for the period when the shipyard was owned by Ditchburn & Mare appear to have been deficient. For the period when the yard was operated by Ditchburn & Mare I believe that about 25 per cent of the ships they built did not make an appearance in the Thames Ironworks Historical Catalogue. There are several dates associated with the building of ships, for example the laying down of the keel, the launch date, the completion date and with naval ships, the commission date. So several dates can be ascribed to the vessels, so the dates in this list are just an indication of the approximate date the vessels were completed. Also very often sources give weights and measurements of the ships differently, feet and inches or feet and decimals. I have not tried to get all the dimensions etc. in the same format but have merely recorded the facts listed in the sources.

Ditchburn & Mare, Orchard Shipyard 1838-1847

1838 – *Inkerman*, 365 tons for the Russian government with oscillating engines by John Penn & Son of Greenwich, London.

1838 – *Starlight*, 75 tons for the Iron Steamboat Company. A 82ft x 13.7ft x 6.8ft Thames paddle steamer with oscillating engines by John Penn & Son of Greenwich, London.

1838 – *Daylight*, 75 tons for the Iron Steamboat Company. Thames paddle steamer with oscillating engines by John Penn & Son, Greenwich, London. *Daylight* was the first iron steamboat to be used on the Thames.

1838 – *Moonlight*, 75 tons, for the Iron Steamboat Company. Thames paddle steamer with oscillating engines by John Penn & Son of Greenwich, London.

1838 – *Twilight*, 75 tons for the Iron Steamboat Company. A 83ft x 13.5ft x 6.8ft Thames paddle steamer with oscillating engines by John Penn & Son of Greenwich, London.

1839 – *Bride*, 100 tons for the Iron Steamboat Company. 93ft 6ins long Thames paddle steamer with oscillating engines by John Penn & Son of Greenwich, London.

1839 – *Bridegroom*, 100 tons for the Iron Steamboat Company. 93.5ft x 13.6ft x 6.9ft Thames paddle steamer with oscillating engines by John Penn & Son of Greenwich, London.

1839 – *Bridesmaid*, 100 tons for the Iron Steamboat Company. Thames paddle steamer with oscillating engines by John Penn & Son of Greenwich, London.

1839 – *Orwell*, 326 tons paddle steamer with 80hp engines for Ipswich Steam Navigation Company.

1840 – *Father Thames*, 120 tons (d), 254 tons, Thames paddle steamer, 141.6ft x 19.2ft x 10ft, built for the Thames Steam Boat Company. Oscillating engines by John Penn & Son of Greenwich, London.

c1840 – *Sons of the Thames*, Thames paddle steamer built for the Thames Steamboat Company. The boat measured 140.6ft x 17ft x 8.3ft.

1840 – *Mermaid*, 123 tons (d), Thames paddle steamer, 120ft x 16ft, with rotary engine designed by Galloway.

1840 – *Queen Elizabeth*, 317 tons (d), wooden paddle steamer cargo ship, 135ft long, Prussian Post Office packet.

1840 – *Pluto*, paddle steamer for the Indian Navy with 200ihp, 40in x 4ft oscillating engines by Maudslay of London.

1840 – *Proserpine*, paddle steamer for Indian Navy with 180ihp, 38ins x 3ft 6ins oscillating engines by Maudslay of London.

1840 – *Propeller,* Thames paddle steamer. The paddles consisted of single blades of iron dipping almost perpendicularly into the water and being forced backwards by an iron arm, making her action like a grasshopper. The ship was built for the Blackwall Railway Company.

1840 – *Stephen*, paddle steamer for Swiss Lakes.

1840 – *Ludwig*, paddle steamer for Swiss Lakes.

1840 – *Cardinal Wolsey*, Thames paddle steamer, 106ft long, engines by Braithwaite & Milner. She worked between London, Richmond and Hampton Court.

1840 – *Locomotive*. A 100ft long paddle steamer for the Thames. Engines by Braithwaite & Milner She worked between London, Richmond and Hampton Court.

1840 – *Triton*, 358 tons for the General Steam Navigation Company, paddle steamer. Scrapped 1878.

1840 – *Lotus*, Nile paddle steamer with oscillating paddle engines by John Penn & Son of Greenwich, London. Built for the Peninsular & Oriental Company.

1841 – *Brunswick*, 126 tons (d), Thames paddle steamer 146ft x 19ft, for the Blackwall Railway Company. 90hp direct engines by Seawards.

1841 – *Blackwall*, 126 tons (d), 158ft long Thames paddle steamer, 146ft x 19ft. Steeple engine by Miller & Ravenhill.

1841 – *Satellite*, 101 tons (d), passenger ship, 139ft 10ins x 17ft x 8ft 4ins.

1841 – *Eagle*, 195 tons (d), passenger ship, 182ft x 21ft 1in, paddle steamer.

1841 – *Railway*, 126 tons (d), passenger ship, paddle steamer with 90hp engines by John Penn & Son of Greenwich, London. This 146ft x 19ft x 10ft ship was built for the Blackwall Railway Company.

1841 – *Waterman* (1-4), four 29 tons (d), passenger ships, 96ft x 13ft 9ins, Thames paddle steamers with oscillating engines by John Penn & Son of Greenwich, London.

1841 – *Cairo*, 26 tons (d), passenger ship, 101ft x 14ft 1in, to convey passengers and luggage to and from various places on the Nile. Oscillating engines by John Penn & Son of Greenwich, London.

1841 – *Courier*, a ship built to navigate the Elbe from Hamburg to Magdeburg. Oscillating engines by John Penn & Son of Greenwich, London. The ship measured 138ft x 20ft x 19ins draught.

1841 – *Emu*, paddle steamer built in sections and rebuilt in Australia for the Parramatta Steam Co. Sydney.

1841 – *Sapphire*, 184 tons (d), cargo ship, paddle steamer with direct acting engines with open top cylinders (100nhp). This 145ft ship was constructed for the Diamond Steam Packet Company

1841 – *Mystery*, 25 tons racing yacht for Lord Alfred Paget.

1841 – *Comet*, paddle steamer, later renamed *Granville*. The ship measured 143.2ft x 19.2ft x 9.4ft. Scrapped in 1873.

1841 – *Swallow*, ship intended for the Baltic, oscillating engines by John Penn of Greenwich, London.

1841 – *Elberfeld*, ship intended for the Rhine, paddle oscillating engines by Miller & Ravenhill of London.

1841 – *Meteor*, paddle steamer, London to Medway. A 274 ton ship built for the Star Steam Packet Company with engines by Miller and Ravenhill.

1841 – *Helvetia*, paddle steamer for Lake Geneva, Switzerland.

1841 – *Ferdinand 2nd*, wooden paddle warship for Neapolitan Navy.

1841 – *Neptune*, wooden paddle warship for Neapolitan Navy.

1841 – *Infant Princess,* small paddle steamer for Thomas Waghorn for use on the Nile.

1841 – Luggage boat, paddle steamer for Thomas Waghorn for use on the Nile. The ship measured 55ft x 11ft x 3ft 6ins.

1842 – *Flirt*, 43 tons (d), passenger ship, 104ft x 13ft 5ins.

1842 – *Waterman* (5). 106ft ship.

1842 – *Waterman* (7&8), 72 tons (d), Thames paddle steamers with oscillating engines by John Penn & Son of Greenwich, London.

1842 – *Coquette,* 43 tons (d), passenger ship.

1842 – Tugs (1-3), 56 tons (d), 80ft x 14ft, for Rome, they were named *Archimede, Blasco de Garay* and *Papin,* they were built for the Papal States with engines by Seaward & Capel.

1842 – *Magician*, 176 tons (d), cargo ship, 148ft 7ins x 21ft 3ins, paddle steamer. 41ins x 3ft 6ins oscillating paddle engines by John Penn of Greenwich, London. This ship was built for the General Steam Navigation Company.

1842 – *Bluebell*, 20 tons (d), yacht, 44ft x 12ft.

1842 – *Echo*, 37 tons (d), passenger ship, 100ft x 13ft.

1842 – *Matrimony*, 50 tons Thames paddle steamer with 22ins x 2ft oscillating engines by John Penn & Son, Greenwich, London. Built for the Iron Steam Boat Company. The measurements of this ship were 95ft x 13.4ft x 6.4ft.

1842 – *Queen*, 102ft 8ins long for the Greenwich Steam Packet Company.

1842 – *Little Nile*, paddle steamer for the River Nile, engines by John Penn & Son of Greenwich, London.

1842 – *Thames*, paddle steamer for Australia, sixth iron hulled ship to be registered in Australia.

1843 – *South Western*, 180 tons (d), 143ft x 18ft 6ins, for the London and South West Railway Company. Paddle steamer with 36½ins x 3ft side lever engines by Seawards.

1843 – *Herne*, Thames paddle steamer with side lever engines by Boulton & Watt.

1843 – *Waterman* (1 new), 45 tons (d), 107ft x 13ft 9ins, Thames paddle steamer with oscillating engines by John Penn & Son of Greenwich, London.

1843 – *Princess Alice,* 359 tons bm, a paddle steamer, Post Office packet ship with 42½ins x 3ft engines by Maudslay Sons & Field of London. The ship measured 138ft 6ins x 20ft 6ins x 11ft.

1843 – *Wittikind*, 60 tons (d), 134ft 9ins x 13ft 6ins, tug.

1843 – *Wartzburg*, 52 tons (d), 149ft x 13ft 3ins, tug.

1843 – A paddle tug, 59 tons (d).

1843 – *Transit*.

1843 – *Wonder*, 222 (d), tons steamer for the South Western Steam Navigation Company. Engines by Seaward and Capel of London.

1843 – *Heron*, 205 tons (d), 155ft 2ins x 21ft 6ins, cargo ship, paddle steamer.

1843 – *Citta di Roma*, 69 tons (d), 115ft x 15ft, passenger ship, engines by Seaward and Capel of London.

1843 – *Manheim*, 208 tons (d), 170ft x 20ft, Rhine tug with oscillating engines by John Penn & Son of Greenwich, London.

1843 – *Fulminate*, a wooden paddle warship for the Neapolitan Navy.

1844 – *Waterman* (10), 49 tons (d), 197ft x 13ft 6ins, Thames paddle steamer with 25ins x 2ft 6ins oscillating engines by John Penn & Son of Greenwich, London.

1844 – *Waterman* (12), 47 tons (d), 117ft x 13ft 10ins, Thames paddle steamer with oscillating engines by John Penn & Son of Greenwich, London.

1844 – *Princess Royal*, 48 tons (d), 107ft 6ins x 13ft 6ins, passenger ship.

1844 – *Georgian*, 165 tons (d), 87ft 6ins x 26ft, cargo ship.

1844 – *Waterman* (11), 47 tons (d), 117ft 6ins x 13ft 10ins, Thames paddle steamer with oscillating engines by John Penn & Son of Greenwich, London.

1844 – *Princess Mary*, 294 tons (d), 142ft 10ins x 20ft 7ins, passenger ship for the South Eastern Railway Company. A paddle steamer with 42ins x 3ft 6ins engines by Maudslay, Sons & Field of London.

1844 – *Princess Maud*, 294 tons (d), 142ft 10ins x 20ft 7ins, passenger ship for the South Eastern Railway Company. A paddle steamer with 42ins x 3ft 6ins engines by Maudslay, Sons & Field of London.

1844 – *Wonder*, 222 tons (d), passenger paddle steamer, 160ft x 21ft, with Seaward atmospheric engines.

1844 – *Water Lily*, 94 tons (d), 130ft x 17ft, yacht.

1844 – *Wedding Ring*, 50 tons Thames paddle steamer for The Iron Steamboat Company, 97ft x 13.9ft x 6.6ft long with 22ins x 1ft 10ins oscillating engines by John Penn & Son of Greenwich, London.

1845–47 – *Manheim* (2 - 4), 210 tons (d), 173ft x 20ft, Three Rhine tugs with oscillating engines by John Penn & Son of Greenwich, London.

1845 – *Waterman* (13), 48 tons (d), 118ft 3ins x 13ft 11ins, Thames paddle steamer with oscillating engines by John Penn & Son of Greenwich, London.

1845 – *Queen of the Belgians*, 212 tons (d), 155ft x 21ft, cargo ship for the South Eastern Railway Company. A paddle steamer with 42½ins x 3ft 6ins engines by Maudslay, Sons & Field of London.

1845 – *Belvedere*, 19 tons (d), 41ft 10ins x 11ft 6ins, yacht for Mr Fontaine.

1845 – HMS *Harpy*, 344 tons (bm) paddle steamer with 200hp 55ins x 4ft side lever engines by John Penn & Son of Greenwich, London. The ship measured 141ft x 22ft 6ins x 13ft 7ins. Broken up in 1909.

1845 – *Onyx*, 292 tons paddle steamer, Post Office packet ship measuring 139ft x 21ft x ? 44ins x 4ft oscillating engines by John Penn & Son of Greenwich, London.

1845 – HMS *Trident*, 850 tons (bm) paddle steamer sloop, original side lever engines by Maudslay, later replaced by Watt oscillating engines. The ship measured 180ft x 31ft 6ins x 17ft 3ins. Broken up in March 1866.

1845 – HMS *Torch*, 344 tons (bm) paddle steamer with side lever engines by Seawards of London. The ship measured 141ft x 22ft 6ins x 13ft 7ins. Sold out of service in May1856.

1845 – HMS *Myrmidon*, 374 tons (bm) paddle steamer. 48ins x 4ft side lever engines by Watt & Co. The ship measured 141ft x 22ft 6ins x 13ft 7ins. Sold 1858.

1845 – *Violet*, 292 tons paddle steamer. Post Office packet ship with 44ins x 4ft oscillating engines by John Penn & Son of Greenwich, London.

1845 – *Fairy*, 210 tons (d), 146ft x 21ft 1in, screw propelled Queen's Yacht. 42ins x 3ft oscillating screw engines by John Penn of Greenwich, London.

1845 – *Bremen*, 60 tons (d), 141ft 2ins x 13ft 7ins, passenger ship.

1845 – *Levantine*, 400 tons (d), 124ft 7ins x 24ft 5ins, cargo ship.

1845 – *Wezer*, 60 tons (d), 142ft 3ins x 13ft 7ins, passenger ship.

1845 – *Triton*, 477 tons (d), 165ft x 24ft, cargo ship.

1845 – *Queen of the French*, 205 tons (d), 157ft 10ins x 21ft 1in, cargo ship for the South Eastern Railway Company. Paddle engines, 42½ x 3ft 6ins by Maudslay, Sons & Field of London.

1845 – *Pigmy Giant,* intended for government service as a pinnace. Converted to steamboat for experiments, 38ft x 8.6ft x 4ft.

1845 – *Vulcano*, corvette for the navy of Spain with oscillating engines by John Penn & Son of Greenwich, London.

1845 – *Magallenes*, paddle steamer for Spain with oscillating engines by John Penn of Greenwich, London.

1845 – *Anthracite*, Welsh coal steamer.

1845 – Paddle steamer for Mr Zizinis, 147ft 7ins x 21ft 6ins x 7ft 8ins.

1845 – *Rampant Lion*, paddle steamer for Mr Zizinis, 147ft x 21ft 6ins x 7ft 8ins.

1845 – *Geneva*, paddle steamer for Mr Zizinis.

c1845 – Eight tugs for the East India Company.

1846 – *Vesuvio*, paddle steamer for the Italian Government, trading between Naples and Marseilles. The ship was 181ft x 26ft x 16ft 3ins and had 40in x 4ft 6ins paddle engines by Maudslay, Sons & Field of London.

1846 – *Capri*, paddle steamer for the Italian Government, trading between Naples and Marseilles. The ship was 181ft x 26ft 1in x 16ft 2ins with 40in x 4ft 6ins paddle engines by Maudslay, Sons & Field of London.

1846 – *Ionia*, wooden vessel for the Ionian Navy with 42½ x 3ft 6ins paddle engines by Maudslay, Sons & Field of London.

1846 – *Ariel*, 709 tons (d), cargo ship for the Peninsular and Oriental Company. She was laid down in 1845 and launched in 1846. One of the first merchant ships to be built with watertight compartments. *Ariel* was 709 tons gross and 44 tons net. Her measurements were 194ft x 28.3ft x 16ft and her 300ihp oscillating paddle engines were built by John Penn & Son of Greenwich, London, giving an average speed of 9 knots. The ship cost £59,000 and was used on the Malta / Alexandria route. She was taken off this route and was returning to Britain when she was stranded on rocks south of Livorno Lighthouse, Italy on 2nd June 1848. *Ariel* then broke up there in a gale on 1 September 1848.

1846 – *Citizen A – G*, 30 tons (d) 94ft x 13ft 4ins, seven Thames paddle steamers with oscillating engines by John Penn of Greenwich, London.

1846 – *New Starlight*, 30 tons (d), 105ft 6ins x 12ft 6ins, passenger ship, 94ft long.

1846 – *Bee*, 32 tons (d) 111ft 6ins x 14ft, Thames paddle steamer built for the Dyer's Hall Company. Compound oscillating engines by Joyce & Co.

1846 – *Ant*, 32 tons (d), 111ft 6ins x 14ft, Thames paddle steamer built for the Dyer's Hall Company. Compound oscillating engines by Joyce & Co.

1846 – *Lady Of The Lake*, 30 tons (d), 105ft 6ins x 12ft 6ins, passenger ship.

1846 – *Starlight*, 30 tons (d) 105ft 6ins x 12ft 6ins, Thames paddle steamer.

1846 – *Lalla Rookh*, 31 tons (d), Thames paddle steamer with oscillating engines by John Penn of Greenwich, London. The ship measured 106.8ft x 12.4ft x 6.1ft.

1846 – HMS *Recruit*, 462 tons (d), 113ft x 30ft 6ins, iron sailing brig.

1846 – *Childe Harold*, 31 tons (d), 107ft x 12ft 6ins, passenger ship.

1846 – *Waverly*, 31 tons (d), 111ft x 12ft 6ins, Thames paddle steamer, 109ft x 12.6ft x 6.2ft, 24nhp oscillating engines by John Penn & Son of Greenwich, London.

1846 – *Rose*, 160 tons (d), 125ft 3ins x 21ft 4ins, cargo ship. London to Dublin screw steamer with engines by Maudslay, Sons & Field of London.

1846 – *Pearl*, 160 tons (d), 125ft 3ins x 21ft 4ins, cargo ship, London to Dublin with 25ins x 2ft screw engines by Maudslay, Sons & Field of London.

1846 – *Volcano*, 500 tons (d), 165ft 2ins x 28ft 11ins, cargo ship.

1846 – *City of Rotterdam*, 304 tons (d), cargo/passenger ship with 90ihp engines by Maudslay, Sons & Field of London. Two cylinders 25ins x 2ft. Built for the London, Rotterdam & Harlingen Steam Schooner Shipping Company and then taken over by the General Screw Steam Shipping Co. The ship measured 110ft 1ins x 23ft 1in.

1846 – *City of London*, 304 tons (d), cargo/passenger ship with 90ihp engines by Maudslay, Sons & Field of London. Two cylinders 25ins x 2ft. Built for the London, Rotterdam & Harlingen Steam Schooner Shipping Company and then taken over by the General Screw Steam Shipping Co. The ship measured 110ft 1in x 23ft 1in.

1846 – *Chemin de Fer*, a cross channel paddle steamer with engines by Maudslay, Sons & Field, for the Belgian Railway Co.

1846 – *Lord John Russell*, screw steamer for the London, Rotterdam & Harlingen Steam Schooner Shipping Company and then taken over by the General Screw Steam Shipping Company. Two 26ins x 2ft 2ins engines by John Penn & Son of Greenwich, London. The ship measured 120.4ft x 22.8ft x 11.9ft. Converted to a hulk in 1886.

1846 – *Times*, 193 tons (d), cargo ship.

1846 – HMS *Sharpshooter*, 585 tons (d), gunboat with 202hp engines.

1846 – Dredger, 113 tons (d), dredger.

1846 – *Cricket*, 47 tons (d), Thames paddle steamer for the Dyer's Hall Company with compound oscillating engines by Joyce & Co.

1846 – *Erin*, 1,065 tons (d), cargo ship for the Peninsular and Oriental Company. Gross tonnage given as 798 and 533 tons net. The ship was 199ft x 27.5ft x 17.1ft with Maudslay, Sons & Field, 280ihp. 45ins x 5ft paddle engines. She was used on the Southampton to the Black Sea route later to Calcutta/China. Stranded at Calcutta on 6 June 1857.

1846 – *Sir Robert Peel*, 396 tons (d), cargo ship with two 26ins x 2ft 6ins oscillating engines by John Penn & Son of Greenwich, London. Built for The London, Rotterdam & Harlingen Steam Schooner Shipping Company and later taken over by The General Screw Steam Shipping Co. The ship measured 125ft x 23ft 4ins. Sold to Boston in 1898.

1846 – *Reina de Castilla* (King of Castille), paddle steamer for Spain with oscillating engines by John Penn & Son of Grenwich, London.

1846 – *Elcano*, paddle steamer for Spain with oscillating engines by John Penn & Son of Greenwich, London.

1846 – *Sybil*, Thames paddle steamer with 25ins x 2ft 3ins oscillating engine by John Penn & Son of Greenwich, London.

1846 – *Ariel*, Post Office packet ship with 64ins x 7ft oscillating paddle engines by John Penn & Son of Greenwich, London. Measurements given as 149 tons and 107ft 11ins x 17ft 3ins x 10ft 3ins.

C.J. Mare, Orchard and Bow Creek Shipyard 1847-1855

1847 – *Norfolk*, 200 tons (d), 151ft 2ins x 21ft 2ins, cargo ship.

1847 – HMS *Antelope*, 857 tons (d), Royal Navy sloop measuring 173ft x 28ft 2ins x 18ft with 64ins x 4ft 6ins oscillating paddle engines by John Penn of Greenwich, London. The Admiralty listed displacement as 1,055tons.

1847 – *Zuleta's* Wooden Boat, 514 tons (d), 143ft x 25ft 4ins, cargo ship.

1847 – *Waterman* No. 7, 33 tons (d), Thames paddle steamer, 108ft x 13ft 4ins, 32nhp engines.

1847 – *Zulueta's* Iron Boat, 112 tons (d), 140ft x 18ft, cargo ship.

1847 – *Prince Metternich*, 440 tons (d), 190ft x 25ft 2ins, Rhine tug with oscillating paddle engines by John Penn & Son of Greenwich, London. Newspapers give her as 600 tons with 200hp engines.

1847 – *Prussian Eagle (Preussischer Adler)*, 997 tons (d), 188ft x 31ft, iron dispatch, Prussian Navy 185ft x 31ft x 17ft, oscillating engines by John Penn of Greenwich, London.

1847 – Sardinian vessel (wood), 436 tons (d), 140ft x 21ft 6ins, cargo ship.

1847 – HMS *Sharpshooter*, 489 tons screw steamer for the Royal Navy, she measured 150ft x 26ft 7½ins x 9ft 3ins. with two Miller & Ravenhill 46ins x 3ft horizontal engines.

1847 – *London Pride*, 101.1ft x 13.7ft x 5.6ft Thames paddle steamer with 22ins x 1ft 10ins oscillating engines by John Penn & Son of Greenwich, London.

1847 – *Citizen H-J*, 31 tons (d), Thames paddle steamers, 107ft x 12ft 8ins x 6ft. 4ins, J was slightly longer with 24nhp, 22ins x 1ft 10ins oscillating engines by John Penn & Son of Greenwich, London.

1847 – *Albion*, 473 tons (d), 175ft x 24ft, cargo ship for the General Steam Navigation Company, scrapped 1888.

1847 – *Anglia*

1847 – *Undine*, River Dart paddle steamer, 89.5ftn x 9.4ft x 6.9ft. Broken up in 1864.

1848 – *Vladimir*, 1,680 tons (d), 200ft x 35ft 7ins, paddle sloop for the Russian Government, 400hp oscillating engines by Rennie of London.

1848 – *Caradoc*, 591 tons (d), Post Office packet, paddle steamer with direct engines by Seaward of London. Built for the Holyhead station but commissioned as a gunboat during the Crimean War. Sold out of service in 1870.

1848 – *Express*, 275 tons (d), cargo/passenger ship for the London and South Western Railway Company. A paddle steamer, 159ft x 21ft x ? with annular 54ins x 3ft 6ins engines by Maudslay, Sons & Field of London.

1848 – *Despatch*, 306 tons (d), cargo/passenger ship for the London and South Western Railway Company. A paddle steamer, 165ft x 23ft, with annular 54ins x 3ft 6ins engines by Maudslay, Sons & Field of London.

1848 – *Courier*, 306 tons (d), cargo/passenger ship for the London and South Western Railway Co. A paddle steamer, 165ft x 23ft, with annular 54ins x 3ft 6ins engines by Maudslay, Sons & Field of London.

1848 – *Rigi*, paddle steamer for Lake Lucerne with oscillating engines by John Penn & Son of Greenwich, London.

1848 – *Danube*, 110 tons (d), 160ft x 18ft, cargo/passenger ship.

1848 – *Citizen K to N*, 32 tons (d), four Thames paddle steamers, 103.5ft x 12.3ft x 6.4ft with 24nhp oscillating paddle engines by John Penn & Son of Greenwich, London.

1848 – Sardinian tug, 157 tons, (d).

1848 – Admiralty tug, 97 tons (d).

1848 – Russian tug, 96 tons (d), 100ft x 16ft 6ins.

1848 – *Enicole*, 600 tons (d), 180ft x 26ft, cargo ship.

1848 – *Mosquito*, 60 tons (d), 49ft x 15ft 4ins, sailing yacht for Lord Alfred Paget.

1849 – *Hellespont*, 643 tons (d), cargo iron steamer, General Screw Steam Shipping Company. A screw steamer with 300hp 36ins x 2ft engines by Maudslay, Sons & Field of London. The ship measured 175ft x 25ft. Sunk in 1863 after a collision with a French steamer.

1849 – *Bosphorus*, 643 tons (d), cargo iron steamer for the General Screw Steam Shipping Company. The ship was 175ft x 25ft. A screw steamer with 80hp twin cylinder diagonal engines 36ins x 2ft by Maudslay, Sons & Field of London. Wrecked at Zitzikamma Point, Cape Colony in 1867. Later converted to a barque and lost in 1882.

1849 – HMS *Vulcan*, 2,396 tons bm, 220ft x 41ft, iron screw frigate with horizontal 49½ins x 2ft engines by J.&G. Rennie of London. The ship measured 220ft x 41ft 5ins x 15ft 6ins.

1849 – *Uncle Sam*, Thames paddle tug for Wm.Watkins, 120ft x 20ft. This veteran ship survived until 1900 when she was sold to Dutch shipbreakers.

1849 – *Rhine*, 584 tons (d), 190ft x 26ft 6ins, cargo/passenger steamer built for the General Steam Navigation Company. Scrapped 1889.

1849 – *Propontis*, 643 tons (d), cargo iron steamer, for the General Screw Steam Shipping Co. two 40hp direct 36ins x 2ft screw engines by Maudslay, Sons & Field of London. The ship measured 175ft x 25ft x 15ft.5ft. Sold to Russia in 1856.

1850 – HMS *Highflyer*, 1,738 tons (d), 192ft x 36ft, guard ship, 55ins x 2ft 6ins screw engines by Maudslay, Sons & Field of London.

1850 – *Francisco d'Asisi*, 2,818 tons (d), 230ft x 36ft 9ins, wooden paddle sloop for the Spanish government with 57¼ins x 7ft engines by Maudslay, Sons & Field.

1850 – *Isabel Secunda*, 2,818 tons (d), 230ft x 36ft 9ins, wooden paddle sloop for the Spanish government with 57¼ins x 7ft engines by Maudslay, Sons & Field.

1850 – *Graf Vorontsov*, a Russian Tug, 73 tons (d), 90ft x 16ft, with oscillating paddle engines by John Penn & Son of Greenwich, London.

1850 – *Peterhoff*, 218 tons (d) 181ft x 21ft 7ins, cargo ship.

1851 – *Panther*, 500 tons (d), 182ft cargo ship, General Steam Navigation Company.

1851 – *Harbinger*, 1,486 tons (d), cargo ship for the General Screw Steam Shipping Company. Built in 1846 by Ditchburn & Mare as HMS *Recruit* as an iron sailing vessel. Lengthened and converted to screw with 150hp 41½ins x 2ft 3ins, Maudslay, Sons & Field diagonal direct engines. Condemned in 1860 at Port Elizabeth, South Africa.

1851 – *Queen of the South*, 2,588 tons (d), 240ft x 39ft, cargo ship, General Screw Steam Shipping Company, screw steamer with two inclined direct acting 55ins x 2ft 6ins engines by Maudslay, Sons & Field of London. Wrecked on Ocean Beach, New York in 1885.

1851 – *Faid Gihaa*d, 2,929 tons (d), 282ft x 40ft, paddle yacht for the Viceroy of Egypt. 2,343ihp, 68ins x 9ft engines by Maudslay of London.

1851 – *Queenstown*, 58 tons (d), 114ft x 14ft 8ins, paddle passenger ship with 25ins x 2ft 4ins oscillating engines by John Penn & Son of Greenwich, London. Ship built for the Cork, Blackrock and Passage Railway.

1851 – *Ravensbourne*, 789 tons (d), 195ft x 27ft, cargo ship.

1851 – *Lady Jocelyn*, 2,588 tons (d), screw steamer built for the General Screw Steam Shipping Company with 55ins x 2ft 6ins diagonal direct 300hp engines by Maudslay, Sons & Field of London. The ship measured 240ft x 39ft. Sold to Dutch shipbreakers in 1922.

1852 – *Mauritius*, 2,563 tons, cargo ship for General Screw Steam Shipping Company. Two engines by James Watt & Co. of Birmingham. The ship measured 244.5ft x 38.1ft x 25.4. The ship was wrecked in 1892 near Cardiff under the Norwegian flag.

1852 – *Hydaspes*, 2,563 tons (d), cargo ship for the General Screw Steam Shipping Company. Screw steamer with horizontal 55ins x 3ft engines by James Watt & Co. of Soho. The ship measured 246ft x 39ft. Sank off Dungeness in 1880.

1852 – *Indiana*, 2,588 tons (d), General Screw Steam Shipping Company, screw steamer with 300hp diagonal direct 55ins x 2ft 6ins engines by Maudslay, Sons & Field of London. The ship measured 240ft x 39ft. Probably sunk by an explosion off the coast of Australia in 1876.

1852 – *Calcutta*, 2,563 tons (d), cargo ship for the General Screw Steam Shipping Company, a screw steamer with 300hp, 55ins x 2ft direct acting engines by Maudslay, Sons & Field of London. The ship measured 244.5ft x 38.1ft x 25.4ft. Foundered in 1887 after a collision.

1853 – *Alexandroff*, 218 tons (d) 181ft x 21ft 7ins, cargo ship.

1853 – *Victoria*, passenger paddle steamer, 135ft x 15ft 6ins, with 29ins x 2ft 9ins oscillating engines by John Penn of Greenwich, London. Ship built for the Cork, Blackrock and Passage Railway.

1853 – *Himalaya*, 3,947 tons (d), cargo/passenger ship for the Peninsular and Oriental Company. Laid down initially as a paddle steamer but completed with a screw. Her measurements were 372.9ft x 46.2ft x 34.9ft with a gross tonnage of 3,438 and a net of 2,327. Single screw powered by 2,050ihp, 84½ins x 3ft 6ins direct acting horizontal trunk steam engine by John Penn & Son of Greenwich, London. Reduced to a hulk. Bombed and sunk in Portland Harbour by German aircraft in 1940.

1853 – *Sea Mew*, 302 tons (d), 143ft x 22ft cargo and passenger vessel.

1853 – *San Giovanni*, 81 tons (d), 98ft 3ins x 16ft 4ins, tug.

1853 – *Tiber*, 68 tons (d),122ft 6ins x 15ft, tug.

1853 – *Victoria*, 84 tons (d), 122ft 6ins x 15ft, tug.

1853 – *Argo*, 2,563 tons (d), cargo ship for the General Screw Steam Shipping Company, screw steamer with 300hp diagonal direct 55ins x 2ft 6ins engines by Maudslay, Sons & Field of London. The ship measured 244.5ft x 38.4ft x 25.5ft. Wrecked in Trepassey Bay.

1853 – *Moselle*, 646 tons (d), 200ft x 26ft 6ins, cargo ship for General Steam Navigation Company. Scrapped 1888.

1853 – *Dragon Fly*, 43 tons (d), 57ft x 11ft 9ins, tug.

1853 – *Nagler*, 564 tons (d), 180ft x 25ft 6ins, cargo ship for the Rhine.

1853 – *Valetta*, 944 tons (d), wooden cargo/passenger ship for P&O. The records give the dimensions of the ship as 225ft x 27.5ft x 17ft with a gross tonnage of 900 and a net of 571. It was a paddle ship with 1,027ihp, 72ins x 7ft oscillating steam engines by John Penn & Sons of Greenwich, London.

1853 – *Guadalquivir*, 169 tons (d), 165ft x 19ft 6ins, passenger ship.

1853 – *Guadalope*, 169 tons (d), 165ft x 19ft 6ins, passenger ship.

1853 – *Croesus*, 3,335 tons (d), cargo ship for the General Screw Steam Shipping Company. Screw engines, 400hp by G.&J. Rennie of London. The ship measured 280ft x 41.5ft x 31.7ft. Destroyed by fire in 1855 off Portofino in the Gulf of Genoa.

1853 – *Jason*, 3,335 tons (d), screw cargo ship for the General Screw Steam Shipping Company. Twin cylinder horizontal direct acting 64ins x 3ft engines by James Watt & Co. of Soho. The ship measured 278.5ft x 42.1ft x 31ft. Stranded off Madras 1862.

1853 – *Natal*, 679 tons (d), cargo ship. Three masted schooner rigged iron sailing ship built for the General Screw Steam Shipping Company. The ship measured 183ft 5ins x 25.7ft x 14.5ft. In 1855 she became stranded on the Spanish coast and became a total wreck.

1853 – *Rajah*, 878 tons (d) auxiliary collier ship for the P&O. Measurements given are 163.6ft x 24ft x 16.7ft with gross tonnage of 600 and net of 419. The ship had a single screw powered by a 120ihp trunk geared steam engine by James Watt & Co. of Birmingham. Sunk in collision in 1875.

1853 – *Freyer*, 185 tons (d), 150ft x 18ft 6ins, cargo paddle steamer for the Rhine. The ship measured 150ft x 18ft 6ins x 10ft 5½ins.

1853 – *Manilla*, 998 tons (d) collier for the Peninsular and Oriental Company. The ship's measurements were 178ft x 26ft x 18.6ft with a gross tonnage of 646 and 503 net. Her single screw was driven by a 290ihp trunk geared steam engine built by Day, Summers & Co. of Southampton.

1853 – *Golden Fleece*, 3,335 tons (d), cargo ship for the General Screw Steam Shipping Co. with 300hp, 55ins x 2ft 6ins diagonal direct screw engines by Maudslay, Son & Field of London. The ship measured 280ft x 42.3ft x 33ft. Sank off Penarth in 1869.

1854 – *Candia*, 2,548 tons (d), cargo/passenger ship for the Peninsular and Oriental Company. The company's records give the dimensions as 281ft x 38.9ft x 26.2ft with a gross tonnage of 2,200 with 989 net. She has a single screw driven by a 1,490ihp geared 71ins + 71ins x 4ft trunk steam engine built by J.&G. Rennie & Co Ltd of London. Sold to Japanese shipbreakers in 1893.

1854 – *Guillaume Tell*, 73 tons (d), 130ft x 14ft, passenger ship.

1854 – *Cape Of Good Hope*, 679 tons (d), cargo. An iron schooner with auxiliary screw engines built for the General Screw Steam Shipping Co. The engines were 41ins x 3ft oscillating engines made by Seaward of London. The ship measured 191.5ft x 26.3ft x 15.3ft. Sank in 1859 after a collision with the *Nemesis* at the mouth of the River Hooghly.

1854 – *Fairy*, 36 tons (d), 96ft x 13ft 6ins, yacht.

1854 – *Woronzoff*, 74 tons (d), 75ft x 16ft, passenger ship.

1854 – For New Zealand, 56 tons (d), 90ft x 14ft, passenger ship.

1854 – For New Zealand, 56 tons (d), 90ft x 14ft, passenger ship.

1854 – *Harlingen*, 610 tons (d), cargo ship for the General Screw Steam Shipping Company, 50hp engines by the Neath Abbey Iron Company. The ship measured 174ft x 25ft x 13.6ft. Reported to be in Constantinople in 1920 and sold in 1923.

1854 – *Industry*, 998 tons (d), 178ft x 27ft, cargo ship.

1854 – Mortar Floats, 340 tons (bm).

1854 – HMS *Urgent*, 2,420 tons (bm), 273ft x 38ft 4ins, despatch vessel.

1854 – HMS *Perseverance*, 2,240 tons (bm), 273ft x 38ft 4ins, despatch vessel.

1854 – HMS *Transit*, 2,775 tons (bm), 302ft x 41ft 8ins, transport with trunk engine by John Penn & Son of Greenwich, London.

1854 – HMS *Arrow*, 1,420 tons (bm), 160ft x 25ft, despatch vessel.

1854 – HMS *Beagle*, 1,420 tons (bm), 160ft x 25ft, despatch vessel.

1854 – HMS *Lynx*, 1,420 tons (bm), 160ft x 25ft, despatch vessel with 35ins + 35ins x 1ft 8ins trunk engine by John Penn of Greenwich, London.

1854 – HMS *Snake*, 1,420 tons (bm), 160ft x 25ft, despatch vessel with 35ins + 35ins x 1ft 8ins trunk engine by John Penn of Greenwich, London.

1854 – *Supply*, 998 tons (d), 178ft x 27ft, cargo ship.

1854 – *Flying Venus*, 2,258 tons (d), 230ft x 37ft 1in, cargo ship.

1854 – *Albert*, 84 tons (d), 135ft x 15ft 6ins, passenger ship with 29ins x 2ft 9ins oscillating paddle engines by John Penn & Son of Greenwich, London. Ship built for the Cork, Blackrock and Passage Railway.

1854 – *Venus*, 161 tons (d), 180ft x 18ft, passenger ship to run between Blackwall and Gravesend. 50hp engines.

1854 – *Illawarra*, 189 tons (d), 106ft x 20ft, cargo and passenger ship.

1854 – *Victor Emmanuel*, 2,097 tons (d), 245ft x 35ft, cargo ship.

1854 – *Conte di Cavour*, 2,097 tons (d), 245ft x 35ft, cargo ship.

1854 – *Standard*, 610 tons (d), 175ft x 25ft 6ins, cargo ship.

1854 – *Queen*, 220 tons (d), 155ft x 20ft, Channel steamer.

1854 – *Empress*, 220 tons (d), 155ft x 20ft, Channel steamer.

1854 – *Europa*, 1,675 tons (d), 225ft x 30ft 6ins, cargo ship.

1854 – *Pilot*, 877 tons (d), 185ft x 28ft cargo vessel for the General Steam Navigation Company.

1854 – *Pioneer*.

1854 – *Pathfinder*.

1854 – *Mutlah*, 439 tons (d), 115ft x 25ft, sailing brig.

1854 – *Fairy*, passenger paddle steamer with 25ins x 1ft 10ins oscillating engines by John Penn of Greenwich, London. Built for the Cork, Blackrock and Passage Railway.

1854 – *Perseverance*, 2,400 tons (d), troopship with screw with 55ins x 3ft trunk engines by John Penn of Greenwich, London.

1854 – *Prince*, auxiliary steam screw ship with barque rig. The ship measured 291ft 5ins x 41ft 6ins x 36ft 8ins. 815ihp engines by Maudslay of London. Foundered in the Black Sea in 1854. Wreck discovered by archaeologists in 2010.

1855 – *Pera*, 2,862 tons (d), cargo/passenger ship, Peninsula and Oriental Company. Originally laid down as *Sobraon*. Her measurements are recorded as 334ft x 42.3ft x 27.2ft with a tonnage of 2,126 gross and 1,261 net. Her single screw was powered by a 1,373ihp trunk geared engine by J.&G. Rennie of London. Sank after hitting an iceberg south-west of Cape Race, 1882.

1855 – *C.J. Mare*, 412 tons (d), 140ft x 21ft, cargo ship.

1855 – *South Wales*, 1,031 tons (d), 230ft x 28ft, cargo ship.

1855 – Ferry boat, 242 tons (d), 135ft x 26ft, for India.

1855 – Ferry boat, 242 tons (d), 135ft x 26ft, for India.

1855 – *General Victoria*, 829 tons (d), 200ft x 29ft, cargo ship.

1855 – *General Morelos*, 829 tons (d), 200ft x 29ft, cargo ship.

1855 – *Hadgier Barbier*, 40 tons (d), 85ft x 10ft, yacht.

1855 – *Teir Neil*, 30ft x 5ft, launch.

1855 – *Torino*, 2,607 tons (d), 263ft x 38ft, cargo ship for Italy.

1855 – HMS *Blazer*, 65ft x 20ft 6ins, mortar vessel.

1855 – HMS *Mastiff*, 65ft x 20ft 6ins, mortar vessel.

1855 – HMS *Nightingale*, 309 tons (bm) 106ft x 21ft 8ins, Dapper class gunboat with two horizontal engines (200hp) by Maudslay, Sons & Field of London.

1855 – HMS *Meteor*, 700 tons (bm), 172ft 6ins x 43ft 5ins, wooden floating battery with 530hp engines by Maudslay, Sons & Field of Greenwich, London.

1855 – HMS *Thunder*, 700 tons (bm), 172ft 6ins x 43ft 5ins, wooden floating battery.

1855 – *Alliance*, paddle steamer with 62ins x 4ft 6ins atmospheric engines by Seaward of London. The ship measured 175.6ft x 23.8ft x 16.7ft.

Thames Iron Works, Orchard and Bow Creek Shipyard from 1856 to 1912

1856 – *Genova*, 2,607 tons (d), 263ft x 38ft, cargo ship for Italy, 866hp screw engines by Maudslay, Sons & Field of London.

1856 – HMS *Bouncer*, 309 tons (bm), 106ft x 21ft 8ins, gunboat 'Albacore' class with 21ins + 21ins x 1ft trunk engine by John Penn & Son of Greenwich, London.

1856 – HMS *Hyaena*, 309 tons (bm), 106ft x 21ft 8ins, gunboat 'Albacore' class with 21ins + 21ins trunk engine by John Penn & Son of Greenwich, London.

1856 – HMS *Violet*, 309 tons (bm), 106ft x 21ft 8ins, gunboat 'Albacore' class with two horizontal engines by Maudslay, Sons & Field of Greenwich, London.

1856 – HMS *Wolf*, 309 tons (bm), 106ft x 21ft 8ins, gunboat, 'Albacore' class with two horizontal engines by Maudslay, Sons and Field.

1856 – HMS *Savage*, 309 tons (bm), 106ft x 21ft 8ins, gunboat 'Albacore' class with trunk engine by John Penn of Greenwich, London.

1856 – HMS *Reynard*, 605 tons (d), 180ft x 28ft, 'Vigilant' class gun vessel.

1856 – HMS *Foxhound*, 605 tons (d), 180ft x 28ft.

1856 – *Dolphin*, 936 tons (d), 195ft x 28ft 1in, cargo ship for General Steam Navigation Company.

1856 – *Fire Float*, 60 tons (d), 193ft x 14ft 6ins.

1856 – *Havre*, 650 tons (d), 185ft 6ins x 23ft 10ins, paddle cargo ship with diagonal engines with open top cylinders by Seaward & Capel of London (launched in 1855).

1857 – *Prince Frederick William*, 249 tons (d), 165ft x 20ft, Dover mail steamer.

1857 – *Wolf*, 702 tons (d), 176ft x 24ft, cargo ship.

1857 – *Fantasie*, 252 tons (d), 180ft x 18ft, passenger ship.

1858 – *St Paul*, 67 tons (d), 85ft x 14ft, tug.

1858 – *St Peter*, 79 tons (d), 107ft x 15ft 6ins, tug.

1858 – *Parramatta*, 5,060 tons (d), 330ft x 43ft 9ins, paddle steamer for the Royal Mail Steam Packet Company.

1858 – *Seine*, 5,060 tons (d), 330ft x 43ft 9ins, paddle steamer for Royal Mail Steam Packet Company.

1858 – *Vulcan*, 166 tons (d), 100ft x 19ft, tug.

1858 – *Emeralde*, 250 tons (d), 150ft x 19ft 2ins, paddle cargo ship for Belgian State Railways.

1859 – *Nepaul*, 1,335 tons (d), passenger screw steam ship for Peninsular and Oriental Company. Her measurements are recorded as 244ft x 29.7ft x 18ft. The ship is listed as being 796 tons gross and 541 tons net. The single screw was powered by a 960ihp direct acting inverted steam engine built be Humphrys & Tennant of London.

1859 – *Immacolata Concezione*, 652 tons (d), 178ft x 27ft, corvette for the Pope.

1859 – *Delta*, 2,336 tons (d), passenger paddle steamer for the Peninsular and Oriental Company. The company records her measurements as 324.2 ft x 35ft x 24.6ft. Her paddles were driven by 1,612ihp oscillating steam engines built by John Penn & Son of Greenwich, London. P&O listed her as 1,618 gross tonnage and 1,020 net. Sold to Japan. Sailed from Muroran to San Francisco in 1906 but never arrived. In 1913 she was seen by a Russian expedition abandoned and locked in ice north of Sakhalin.

1859 – *Sextant*, 288 tons (d), 130ft x 20ft, tug.

1859 – *Ly-ee-Moon*, 1,318 tons (d), 270ft x 27ft 3ins, opium clipper for Dent & Co. Converted to screw steamer in 1874, sank 1886.

1860 – *John Penn*, 259 tons (d), 170ft x 20ft, Channel paddle steamer for LC&D Railway Company. Oscillating paddle engines by John Penn of Greenwich, London.

1860 – HMS *Warrior*, 9,137 tons ironclad broadside ship with a 5,267ihp engine built by John Penn & Son of Greenwich, London. This was a horizontal single expansion trunk engine driving a single screw. *Warrior* measured 420ft x 58ft 4ins x 26ft. Preserved at Portsmouth.

1860 – *Oberon*, 16 tons (d), 38ft x 7ft 6ins, yacht.

1860 – Unknown, 10 tons (d), 52ft x 7ft 6ins yacht.

1860 – *Valiente*, screw gunboat for Spain with trunk engines by John Penn & Son, Greenwich, London.

1860 – *Velindra*, paddle steamer with oscillating engines. The ship measured 158.4ft x 19.1ft x 9.1ft. Scrapped in 1897.

1860 – *Mooltan*, 3,091 tons (d), passenger steamer for the Peninsula and Oriental Company. Her measurements were 348.8ft x 39.1ft x 28.7ft. She had a single screw driven by a pair of tandem compound inverted direct acting steam engines of 1,734ihp made by Humphrys, Tennant & Co. of London. Disappeared without trace in North Atlantic in 1891.

1861 – *Lord of the Isles*, 117 tons (d), 130ft x 18ft, passenger ship with oscillating paddle engines by John Stewart & Sons of London.

1861 – *Sunbeam*, 125 tons (d), 85ft 6ins x 16ft, yacht.

1861 – *Lady of the Lake*, 121 tons (d), 140ft x 18ft, passenger ship with oscillating paddle engines by John Stewart & Sons of London.

1861 – *Paraguari*, 520 tons (d), 190ft x 26ft, cargo paddle ship for Paraguay.

1862 – *Coonanbara*, 579 tons (d), 210ft x 27ft, cargo paddle ship.

1862 – *Yavari & Yapura*, 115 tons (d), 100ft x 17ft, two gunboats for Peruvian government. Each ship had two 16ins x 1ft 4ins engines manufactured by James Watt & Co. These lake steamers were prefabricated and were assembled on the shores of Lake Titicaca. It took several years for the parts to get to Peru and for the completion of the ships. They were later renamed *Chucuito* and *Puno*. *Yavari* is till preserved on the shores of the lake.

1862 – *Poonah*, 3,080 tons (d), 315ft x 41ft, cargo/passenger ship with screw engines.

1863 – *Morning Star*, 64 tons (d), 150ft x 30ft, yacht.

1863 – *Princess Alexandra*, 581 tons (d), 176ft x 24ft, paddle yacht.

1863 – HMS *Valiant*, Hector Class broadside ironclad. Completed by the Thames Iron Works after the bankruptcy of Westwood & Baillie, horizontal return connecting rod steam engine by Maudslay of London, 3,260ihp. Launched in 1863, completed in 1868 and broken up in 1957. The ship measured 280ft 2ins (pp) x 56ft 3ins x 25ft.

1863 – HMS *Minotaur*, 10,690 tons, ironclad broadside. One shaft, two cylinder horizontal trunk steam engine by John Penn & Son, of London. The ship measured 400ft 3ins pp, 407ft oa x 59ft 6ins x 27ft 9ins. Launched in 1863 and completed in 1868. Sold for breaking up in 1922.

1863 – *Absalon*, 527 tons (d), 150ft x 26ft, armoured gunboat, Danish government.

1863 – *Esbernsnare*, 527 tons (d), 150ft x 26ft, armoured gunboat, Danish government.

1863 – *Pervenetz*, 3,277 tons (d), 220ft x 53ft, armoured warship, Russian government. One shaft horizontal direct acting screw steam engines of 1,200ihp by Maudslay, Sons & Field of London. Stricken in 1905.

1863 – *Sultan Mahmoud/Mahmudieh*, 6,400 tons (d), iron hulled broadside ironclad warship, Turkish government. The ship measured 293ft pp x 55ft 9ins x 25ft 7ins max. Discarded 1911.

1863 – *Izzeddin*, 1,218 tons (d), 250ft x 29ft 6ins, cruiser yacht, Sultan of Turkey.

1863 – *Golconda*, 2,843 tons (d), passenger ship, Peninsular and Oriental Company. Her measurements were 314.5ft x 38.3ft x 26.6ft. Her gross tonnage was 1,909 and 1,253 net. Her single screw was driven by a pair of tandem compound inverted direct acting steam engines of 2,112ihp made by Humphrys, Tennant & Dykes of London. Sold in 1881 for breaking up at Bombay.

1864 – *Charkieh*, 2,177 tons (d), 260ft x 35ft, cruiser, Egyptian government, sank 1900.

1864 – *Nyanza*, 2,844 tons (d), a paddle steamer for the Peninsular and Oriental Company. The records of the company give her measurements as 327.3ft x 36.2ft x 27.6ft. Her gross tonnage was listed as 2,082 with net being 1,482. Her paddles were driven by a pair of oscillating steam engines of 2,304ihp built by J.&G. Rennie of London. Sold to India for breaking up in 1904

1864 – *Napoleon III*, 5,759 tons (d), 363ft 6ins x 46ft, mail steamer, France. Renamed later *Ville du Harvre*, rebuilt in 1872 as a screw steamer. Sank in 1873.

1865 – *Tanjore*, 3,069 tons (d), passenger steamer for the Peninsular and Oriental Company. The records of P&O give the gross tonnage as 1,971 with net being 1,389. Her measurements were 321.2ft x 38.1ft x 26.4ft. The ship's engines were built by Ravenhill, Salkeld & Co. of London.

They were tandem compound direct-acting steam engines giving 2,090ihp. The ship was screw driven. Sold to Indian shipbreakers at Bombay in 1894.

1865 – *Vitoria*, 7,135 tons, 316ft 6ins x 56ft 11ins centre battery ironclad built for Spain. One shaft, screw steam engine of 4,500ihp.

1865 – Two tugs, 100ft x 18ft, 152 tons (d).

1866 – *Anglia*, 520 tons (d), 140ft x 22ft, Thames paddle tug for Watkins with side lever engines of 700ihp.

1866 – *Buffalo*, 286 tons, 157.2ft x 21.7ft x 11.9ft, compound engines, torpedoed in 1918.

1866 – HMS *Serapis*, 6,120 tons Euphrates class troopship 360ft x 49ft with four cylinder compound engine.

1867 – HMS *Waterwitch*, 1,280 tons armoured gunboat. Ruthven hydraulic turbine, experimental. The ship measured 162ft pp x 32ft 1in x11ft 11ins. Launched in 1866 and completed in 1867. Sold in 1890.

1867 – *Basileos Georgios*, 1,775 tons (d), 200ft x 23ft, armour clad small central battery ship, Greek government. The ship measured 200ft pp x 33ft x 16ft max.

1867 – *La Poste*, 101 tons (d), 100ft x 20ft, tug.

1867 – Iron tank vessel, 60ft x 20ft.

1868 – *Anchor Hoy*, 90 tons (d), 64ft x 19ft.

1869 – *Avni Illah*, 2,314 tons (d), casemate ironclad for the Turkish government. One shaft horizontal compound screw steam engine, 2,200ihp. The ship measured 226ft 4ins x 36ft x 16ft 5ins max.

1869 – *John Penn*, 366 tons (d), 140ft x 22ft 6ins, cargo ship, 21ins x 1ft trunk engines by John Penn & Son of Greenwich, London.

1869 – *Konig Wilhelm*, 9,602 tons (d), armour clad naval ship, Prussian government. One shaft, horizontal single steam engine by Maudslay, Sons & Field of London, 8,440ihp. The ship measured 368ft 1in oa, 356ft 3½ins wl x 60ft x 28ft. Sold in 1921.

1869 – HMS *Active*, 3,080 tons, iron screw corvette. One shaft, horizontal compound steam engine, 2 cylinders by Humphrys & Tennant of London, 4,130ihp. The ship measured 270ft x 42ft x 22ft. Launched in 1869 and completed in 1870. Sold in 1906.

1869 – HMS *Volage*, 3,080 tons, iron screw corvette. One shaft 86ins + 86ins x 3ft 9ins trunk steam engine by John Penn & Son of Greenwich, London, 4,530ihp. Launched in 1869 and completed in 1870. The ship measured 270ft x 42ft x 22ft. Sold in 1904.

1870 – *Fethi Bulend*, 2,720 tons, iron-clad, Turkish government. One shaft, horizontal compound screw steam engine, 3,250ihp. The ship measured 236ft 3ins x 39ft 4ins x 18ft 1in max.

1870 – Ship for the Nile, 54 tons (d), 100ft x 17ft 6ins.

1870 – HMS *Magdala*, 3,344 tons, coast defence monitor. Two shaft with engines by Ravenhill & Salkeld, 1,3691ihp. The ship measured 225ft pp x 45ft x 15ft 4ins. Sold for breaking up in 1904.

1871 – *Kouban*, 733 tons (d), 210ft x 29ft, cargo ship for Russia with 265ihp engines by Maudslay, Sons & Field of London.

1871 – *Terek*, 733 tons (d), 210ft x 29ft, cargo ship for Russia with 310ihp engines by Maudslay, Sons & Field of London.

1871 – *Kodor*, 733 tons (d), 210ft x 29ft, cargo ship for Russia with 300ihp engines by Maudslay, Sons & Field of London.

1871 – HMS *Cyclops*, 3,480 tons, coast defence monitor. Two shaft two cylinder compound steam engines by John Elder of Glasgow, 1,670ihp. The ship measured 225ft pp x 45ft x 16ft 3ins. Launched in 1871 and completed in 1877. Sold for breaking up in 1903.

1872 – Ship for the Nile, 100ft x 17ft 6ins.

1873 – *Castalia*, 1,080 tons (d), 290ft x 17ft, twin hulled passenger vessel with paddle engines by J.&A. Blyth of London.

1874 – HMS *Rover*, 3,460 tons, iron screw corvette. One shaft horizontal compound steam engine by Ravenhill & Salkeld of London, 4,960ihp. The ship measured 280ft x 43ft 6ins x 23ft. Launched in 1874 and completed in 1875. Sold for breaking up in 1893.

1874 – *Messudieh (Mesoudiye)*, 9,120 tons (d), central battery ironclad for the Turkish government. One shaft, horizontal compound screw engine, 7,431ihp by Maudslay, Sons & Field. The ship measured 331ft 5ins x 59ft x 25ft 11ins max. Sunk in1914.

1875 – HMS *Superb*, 9,710 tons, ironclad battery with horizontal direct acting engines by Maudslay, Sons & Field of London. The ship measured 332ft 4ins pp x 59ft x 25ft 6ins. Launched in 1875 and completed in 1880 This ship was designed as *Hamidieh* for Turkey but detained during the Russian war scare. Purchased for the Royal Navy and modified by the Thames Iron Works. Sold for breaking up in 1906.

1876 – *Dom Augusto*, 167 tons (d), 165ft x 18ft, paddle steamer, Portugal.

1877 – *Fox*, 89 tons (d), 75ft x 14ft 6ins, tug.

1877 – *Cleopatra*, special vessel, 92ft x 15ft.

1877 – *Ajax*, 51 tons (d), 60ft x 13ft, tug.

1877 – *Trojan*, 51 tons (d) , 60ft x 13ft, tug.

1877 – *Somtseu*, 115 tons (d), 90ft 17ft 6ins, cargo ship.

1878 – *Purus*, 1,355 tons (d), 250ft x 32ft, paddle troopship for the Brazilian government. This vessel was wood-sheathed and coppered.

1878 – *Vasco da Gama*, 2,479 tons (d), 200ft x 40ft, armour clad for the Portuguese government. Screw compound engine 3,000ihp by Humphrys, Tennant & Dyke of London.

1878 – *Zieten*, 951 tons (d), 226ft x 28ft, torpedo cruiser, German government.

1878 – *Principie Don Carlos*, 435 tons (d), 130ft x 20ft, transport ship, Portuguese government.

1878 – *Sphinx*, 33 tons (d), 65ft x 11ft, torpedo boat, Greek government.

1878 – *Guadiana*, 99 tons (d), customs vessel, Portuguese government, 76ft x 15ft x 7ft.

1878 – *Faro*, 150 tons (d), customs vessel, Portuguese government, 95ft x 16ft x 8ft.

1878 – *Tejo*, 229 tons (d), customs vessel, Portuguese government, 108ft x 17.6ft x 2.6ft.

1878 – Unknown, 31 tons (d), 82ft x 10ft, experimental brass torpedo boat.

1878 – *Hawk*, 53 tons (d), 60ft x 13ft, tug.

1878 – *Stour,* 107 tons (d), 125ft x 17ft 6ins, Thames paddle steamer, Great Eastern Railway.

1878 – *Enterprise*, 50 tons (d), 62ft x 13ft, tug.

1878 – *Imperial*, 86 tons (d), 75ft x 15ft, paddle steamer Great Eastern Railway.

1879 – *Middlesex*, 112 tons (d), 100.3ft x 18.7ft x 7.7ft paddle steamer for the Thames, oscillating engines by Young. Built for the Great Eastern Railway.

1879 – *Queen,* 61 tons (d), 65ft x 13ft 6ins, tug.

1879 – *Canada*, 116 tons (d), 80ft x 17ft, tug.

1879 – *Duke*, 61 tons (d), 65ft x 13ft 6ins, tug.

1879 – *Eonia*, 31 tons (d).

1879 – *Principe de Grao Para*, 431 tons (d), 76ft x 15ft, for Brazil. Paddle 44 x 4ft 6ins oscillating engines by John Penn & Sons of Greenwich, London.

1879 – *Guadiana*, 230 tons (d), 108ft x 17ft 6ins, customs vessel, Portuguese government.

1879 – *Fulminante*, 84 tons (d), 75ft x 15ft, mine layer, Portuguese government.

1879 – *Albion*, 61 tons (d), 65ft x 13ft 6ins, tug.

1879 – *D'Affonso*, 146 tons (d), 158ft x 18ft, paddle steamer, Portugal.

1879 – *Retort*, 78 tons (d), 72ft x 13ft 6ins, tug.

1880 – HMS *Swift*, 788 tons, composite gun vessel of the 'Linnet' class. This ship measured 165ft x 29ft x 10ft 3ins. Engines by John Penn & Sons of Greenwich, London. Sold in 1902.

1880 – HMS *Linnet*, 788 tons, composite gunboat of the 'Linnet' class, dimensions as HMS *Swift*. Sold 1904.

1881 – *Hydra*, later renamed *Ambrakia*, 485 tons (d), 128ft x 26ft 6ins, gunboat for the Greek government with 672ihp engines by Maudslay, Sons & Field of London.

1881 – *Spetsai*, later named *Akteon*, 485 tons (d) 128ft x 26ft 6ins, gunboat for the Greek government.

1881 – *Aghilea*, 84 tons (d), 75ft x 15ft, mine layer, Greek government.

1881 – *Napoleon*, 84 tons (d), 75ft x 15ft, mine layer, Greek government.

1881 – *Monemvassiea*, 84 tons (d), 75ft x 15ft, mine layer, Greek government.

1881 – *Gravina*, 1,139 tons (d), cruiser for the Spanish government. One shaft, horizontal compound screw steam engine, 1,500ihp. The ship measured 210ft pp x 32ft x 13ft 8ins. Lost in 1885.

1881 – *Velasco*, 1,139 tons (d), cruiser, Spanish government. One shaft horizontal compound steam engine, 1,500ihp. The ship measured 210ft pp x 32ft x 13ft 8ins. Sunk in 1898.

1881 – A water boat, 65ft x 17ft.

1881 – *Thames*, 22 tons (d), 80ft x 8ft 9ins, a Thames Conservancy yacht.

1881 – Tug, 54 tons (d), 65ft x 14ft.

1882 – *Mircea*, 390 tons (d), 118ft x 25ft, training brig with screw engines, Romanian government.

1882 – *Rahova*, 53 tons (d), 55ft 6ins x 12ft, a chaloupe for Romania.

1882 – *Smardan*, 53 tons (d), 55ft 6ins x 12ft, a chaloupe for Romania.

1882 – *Opanez*, 53 tons (d). 55ft x 12ft, a chaloupe for Romania.

1882 – *Alexandra cel Brun*, 84 tons (d), mine layer, Romanian government.

1882 – *Invicta*, 1,282 tons (d), 312ft x 33ft 3ins, paddle channel steamer for London, Chatham & Dover Railway Company. Engines (420ihp) by Maudslay, Sons & Field.

1882 – *Norfolk*, 109 tons (d), paddle steamer Great Eastern Railway, later renamed *Onyx*. The ship measured 140ft x 17.5ft x 6.9ft.

1882 – Four paddle steamers, 496 tons (d), 145ft x 17ft, for service on the Brahmaputra River.

1882 – Three cargo flats, 2,514 tons (d), 220ft x 32ft.

1882 – *Lion*, 238 tons (d), 100ft x 19ft 6ins, cargo ship.

1882 – *Dolphin*, 86 tons (d), 75ft x 17ft, tender.

1882 – *Diana*, 58 tons (d), 70ft x 17ft, tug.

1882 – Single screw launch, 43 tons (d), 55ft x 14ft 6ins.

1883 – *Alfonso D' Albuquerque*, 1,112 tons (d), 205ft x 33ft, corvette for the Portuguese government.

1883 – *Anchor Hoy*, 90 tons (d), 64ft x 19ft, iron screw launch.

1883 – Iron screw launch, 68 tons (d), 65ft x 16ft.

1883 – Water boat, 81 tons (d), 65ft x 14ft.

1883 – *Rotifer*, 87 tons (d), 69ft x 14ft, tug.

1883 – *Romulus*, 64 tons (d), 65ft x 12ft 8ins, tug.

1883 – *Remus*, 64 tons (d), 65ft x 12ft 8ins tug.

1884 – *Thrush*, 99 tons (d), 76ft x 15ft, customs vessel, Greek government.

1884 – *Nightingale*, 99 tons (d), 75ft x 15ft, customs vessel, Greek government.

1884 – *Magpie*, 99 tons (d), 75ft x 15ft, customs vessel, Greek government.

1884 – *Alpheos*, 422 tons (d), 130ft x 25ft, gunboat for the Greek government.

1884 – *Achelaos*, 422 tons (d), 130ft x 25ft, gunboat for the Greek government.

1884 – *Emperor*, 63 tons (d), 65ft x 13ft 6ins, tug.

1885 – *Benbow,* 87 tons (d), 70ft x 15ft, tug.

1885 – HMS *Benbow,* 10,600 tons barbette ship. Two shaft three cylinder inverted compound screw steam engines by Maudslay, Sons & Field of London, 10,860ihp. The ship measured 330ft pp x 68ft 6ins x 27ft 10ins, launched in 1885 and completed in 1888. Sold for breaking up in 1909.

1886 – Screw water boat, 93 tons (d), 65ft x 20ft, Indian government.

1887 – *Oltul,* 95 tons (d), 100ft x 13ft 6ins, customs vessel, Romanian government.

1887 – *Siretul,* 95 tons (d) 100ft x 13ft 6ins, customs vessel, Romanian government.

1887 – *Bistrita,* 95 tons (d), 100ft x 13ft 6ins, customs vessel, Romanian government.

1887 – *Regina,* 82 tons (d), 69ft x 14ft, tug.

1887 – *Rodney,* 82 tons (d), 70ft x 15ft, tug.

1887 – *Angel,* 637 tons (d), sailing light.

1887 – *Casilda,* 637 tons (d), 140ft x 28ft 2ins, sailing light.

1887 – *Genara,* 637 tons (d), 140ft x 28ft 2ins, sailing light.

1887 – *Carlos,* 637 tons (d), 140ft x 28ft 2ins, sailing light.

1887 – *Jose,* 637 tons (d), 140ft x 28ft 2ins, sailing light.

1887 – *Ramona,* 637 tons (d), 140ft x 28ft 2ins, sailing light.

1887 – HMS *Sans Pareil,* 10,470 tons, turret ship. Two shaft three cylinder triple expansion screw engines by Humphrys, Tennant & Dyke of London, 14,482ihp. The ship measured 340ft pp, 363ft oa x 70ft x 26ft 9ins. The ship was launched in 1887 and completed in 1891. Sold for breaking up in 1907.

1887 – *Dona Ramona,* 315 tons (d), 140ft x 20ft, paddle tug for Rosario, South America.

1888 – *Marechal MacMahon,* 345 tons (d), 124ft x 21ft, transport, Portuguese Colonial Service in Africa.

1888 – A launch, 26 tons (d), 50ft 2ins x 11ft 2ins, Portugal.

1889 – *Don Amelia,* 150 tons (d), 154ft x 18ft, paddle ship, for the South Eastern Railway of Portugal.

1889 – *Sarmiento,* 105 tons (d), 100ft x 22ft, paddle tug.

1889 – Two saloon paddle steamers for the Chirket-Hairie Company, Turkey, 568 tons (d), 170ft x 21ft, 650hp compound diagonal engines by Maudslay, Sons & Field of London.

1890 – *Limpopo,* 289 tons (d), transport, Portuguese Colonial Service in Africa. The ship measured 124ft x 21ft x 9ft 6ins.

1890 – HMS *Blenheim,* 9,150 tons, protected cruiser first class. Two shaft triple expansion steam engines, 13,000ihp. The ship measured 375ft pp, 399ft 9ins oa x 65ft x 24ft. The ship was launched in 1890 and completed in 1894. Sold in 1926.

1890 – *Woolwich,* 124 tons (d), 100ft x 20ft 6ins, Thames paddle ferry, with oscillating engines by Young & Sons. The ship measured 100ft x 20ft 6ins x 8ft 4ins. Built for the Great Eastern Railway Company.

1892 – *Hilda,* 95 tons (d), 70ft x 2ft 6ins, screw tug.

1892 – HMS *Grafton,* 7,350 tons, protected cruiser First Class. Two shaft, triple expansion steam engines, 12,000ihp. The ship was launched in 1892 and completed in 1894. The ship measured 360ft pp, 387ft 6ins oa x 60ft x 23ft 9ins. Sold in 1920.

1892 – HMS *Theseus,* 7,350 tons, protected cruiser First Class. Two shaft, triple expansion steam engines, 12,000ihp. The ship measured 360ft pp, 387ft 6ins oa x 60ft x 23ft. The ship was launched in 1892 and completed in 1896. Sold in 1921.

1892 – *Coaltar,* 503 tons (d), 107ft x 24ft, sailing tank vessel for Belgium.

1893 – *Coborn,* Thames tug for M. Cohen of London, 16ins + 28ins x 1ft 6ins inverted compound engines by John Penn & Sons of Greenwich, London.

1893 – *Beatrice*, 39tons (d), 77ft x 11ft 6ins, a launch for London County Council with inverted compound 12ins + 23ins x 1ft engine by John Penn & Sons of Greenwich, London.

1894 – *Samoyed*, 983 tons (d), survey vessel, Russian government. The ship measured 170ft x 33ft x 16ft 7ins. Triple expansion inverted compound 21ins + 32ins + 50in x 2ft engines made by John Penn & Sons of Greenwich, London.

1895 – HMS *Zebra*, 310 tons, destroyer. 4,800ihp. She measured 204ft 6ins oa, 200ft pp x 20ft x 7ft 6ins. Launched in 1895 and completed in 1900. Engines by Maudslay, Sons & Field of London. Broken up in 1914.

1895 – Launch 22 & 23 for the Admiralty, high speed with inverted vertical engines by John Penn & Sons of Greenwich, London.

1895 – Launch 143 & 144 for the Admiralty, high speed with inverted vertical engines by John Penn & Sons of Greenwich, London.

1896 – British Ambassador's launch, 29 tons (d).

1896 – *Fuji*, 12,512 tons (d), battleship for the Japanese government. Two shaft vertical triple expansion steam engine, 14,000ihp, by Humphrys, Tennant & Dyke of London. The ship measured 390ft wl, 412ft oa x 73ft x 26ft 3ins. She was laid down in 1894, launched in 1896 and completed in 1897.Scrapped in 1948.

1896 – Pinnaces 337, 338 & 339, 56ft long for the Royal Navy with inverted vertical engines by John Penn of Greenwich, London.

1897 – *Alexandra*, 89 tons (d), 120ft x 17ft, paddle steamer with 23ins x 2ft oscillating engines, built for Thames Steamboat Company.

1897 – Eighteen pinnaces for the Royal Navy, lengths of 40ft or 56ft with inverted vertical engines by John Penn & Sons of Greenwich, London.

1897 – *Boadicea*, 89 tons (d), 120ft x 17ft, steel paddle steamer with 23ins x 2ft oscillating engines, built for Thames Steamboat Company.

1897 – *Cleopatra*, 89 tons (d), 120ft x 17ft, steel paddle steamer with 23ins x 2ft oscillating engines, built for Thames Steamboat Company.

1898 – *Buyukder*, the Russian Ambassador's launch, 26 tons (d), 60ft x 11ft, for service on the Bosphorus.

1898 – *Topeka*, purchased as the *Diogenes*. This ship was launched in 1881 by Howaldt of Kiel. Converted to a naval ship by the Thames Iron Works. Bought by the United States as a patrol gunboat.

1898 – *Shikishima*, 14,850 tons (d), battleship for the Japanese government. Two shaft reciprocating triple expansion steam engines, 14,500ihp by Humphrys, Tennant & Dykes of London. The ship measured 415ft wl, 438ft oa x 75ft 6ins x 27ft 6ins. She was laid down in 1897, launched in 1898 and completed in 1900. Scrapped in 1947.

1898 – HMS *Albion*, 13,150 tons, battleship First Class. Two shaft triple expansion steam engines, 13,500ihp by Maudslay, Sons & Field of London. The ship measured 390ft pp, 421ft 6ins oa x74ft x 26ft 2ins. Launched in 1898 and completed in 1901. Sold for breaking up in 1919.

1898 – Steel boat driven by an oil engine for a party of pioneers to the Klondike.

1901 – HMS *Duncan*, 13,745 tons, battleship First Class. Two shaft four cylinder triple expansion steam engines, 18,000ihp. The ship measured 405ft pp, 432ft oa x 75ft 6ins x 25ft 9ins. Launched in 1901 and completed in 1903. Sold for breaking up in 1920.

1901 – HMS *Cornwallis*, 13,745 tons, battleship First Class. Two shaft four cylinder triple expansion steam engines, 18,000ihp. The ship measured 405ft pp, 432ft oa, x 75ft 6ins x 25ft 9ins. She was laid down in 1899, launched in 1901 and completed in 1904. Torpedoed and sunk by *U32* east of Malta in 1917.

1902 – *Sir Frederick Walker*, 174 tons (d), 93ft 6ins x 18ft 9ins, War Office.

1902 – A screw tug for Portugal, 75 tons (d), 70ft x 15ft.

1902 – *Roding*, 72 tons (d), 68ft x 13ft, launch, Thames Conservancy.

1903 – Screw tug, 50 tons (d), 52ft x 12ft 6ins, War Office.

1904 – Ten paddle steamers for London County Council, 1,260 tons (d). They had 16ins, 31ins x 3ft compound diagonal engines. The ships measured 130ft x 18ft x 6.8ft. They were named *Alleyn, Boydell, Brunel, Carlyle, Gibbon, King Alfred, Morris, Purcell, Sloane* and *Vanbrugh*. These boats were built for service on the Thames but the service was not a success and the boats sold off in 1907.

    Alleyn was sold for £705 to Dundee and finally to Mesopotamia, *Boydell* was sold for £990 to the Royal Servian Privilege Steamship Company, *Brunel* was sold for £500 to J. Parson, Plymouth, *Carlyle* was sold for £990 to Tay Steamboat Company of Dundee, *Gibbon* was sold for £1,000 to K. Bohre, Esschenweg, Rotterdam then resold to Mafalda Soc. Di Nav. A Vao Puglia, Bari, Italy and renamed *Mafalda*. *King Alfred* was sold for £1,050 to Glaser, Brewer & Company, London and then sold to O. May, Memel for service on the Rhine, *Morris* was sold for £393 to the City Steamboat Company, then resold to Germany for service between Cologne and Mulheim, *Purcell* was sold for £980 to the Royal Servian Privilege Steamship Company, *Sloane* was sold for £393 to the City Steamboat Company and then resold to Germany for service on the Rhine and *Vanbrugh* was sold for £990 to Boieldieu Cie Rouennaise de Nav., Rouen.

1904 – Houseboat, Queens College, Oxford

1904 – HMS *Black Prince*, 13,550 tons, armoured cruiser First Class. Two shaft four cylinder triple expansion steam engines, 23,000ihp. The ship measured 480ft pp, 505ft 6ins oa x 73ft 6ins x 26ft. Launched in 1904 and completed in 1906. Sunk in 1916.

1904 – Coaling lighter, 1,571 tons (d), 145ft x 36ft.

1904 – Four barges.

1904 – Eleven lifeboats.

1905 – Two coaling lighters.

1906 – Eight vedette boats 405 tons (d), Romanian government. These were named *Capt Luicar Bogden, Maj Giurascu Dimitriu, Maj Sonstu Gheorge, Maj Nicolae Grigoro Ion, Maj Ena Constatin, Locotenant C Dimitie, Capt Rumano Mihaail* and *Captain Maracineau*. Each had a pair of 9ins + 17ins x 9ins inverted vertical compound engines.

1908 – L 26 A & B, 330 tons (d), 115ft x 18ft, passenger ships for Turkey, named *Ekmet* and *Mesut* with 11ins + 22ins x 1ft 6ins oscillating compound inverted vertical engines by John Penn & Sons of Greenwich, London,

1908 – Five horse boats, 36ft x 10ft 11ins.

1910 – Grab dredging barge, 65 tons (d), 50ft x 22ft.

1910 – HMS *Nautilus*, 1,060 tons (d), 267ft 6ins x 28ft, destroyer with turbine propulsion.

1911 – HMS *Thunderer*, 22,500 tons, battleship. This ship was an Orion class Super-Dreadnought. She was 580ft 9ins x 88ft 6ins x 27ft 6ins. *Thunderer* had quadruple propellers driven by four Parsons steam turbines. Sold for scrapping in 1926.

1911 – Three passenger ships, 1,500 tons (d), for Turkey. Between 1896 and 1911 the Thames Iron Works built 206 lifeboats between 34ft and 43ft long for the Royal National Lifeboat Institution including 11 motor lifeboats. Including these, no less than 250 lifeboats were constructed by the company.

(B) Other Engines Built by The Thames Iron Works

1898 – Triple expansion engine (1,400ihp) for the sloop HMS *Condor*.

1900 – Nineteen engines for pinnaces ordered by the Royal Navy.

1901 – Four cylinder 34ins + 34ins + 54ins + 63ins x 4ft triple expansion compound inverted vertical engines for the battleship HMS *Albemarle* built at Chatham Dockyard.

1905 – Six steam engines for pinnaces ordered by the Royal Navy.

1910 – Steam engine for 50ft pinnace ordered by the Royal Navy.

1911 – Four steam turbines built for HMS *Chatham* being built at Chatham Dockyard.

1911 – Four 14ins + 23ins + 38ins x 2ft 6ins triple expansion steam pumping engines for Walton Waterworks, Metropolitan Water Board.

(C) A Partial List of the Main Civil Engineering Products of The Thames Iron Works.

c1850 – Seven sections for Robert Stephenson's Britannia Railway Bridge over the Menai Straits.

1868 – Sombrero Lighthouse in the Caribbean.

1854 – 1856 - Sections for the Royal Albert Bridge, Saltash.

1862 – Westminster Bridge, London.

1887 – Ironwork for Hammersmith Bridge, London.

1889 – The Royal Pavilion for the Paris Exhibition.

1895 – 1,000 tons of steel girders for an Indian railway bridge, Barking Road Bridge (steel), four swing bridges for the London County Council.

1898 – First span for Kotri Bridge (of 3), Dartford Creek Roof, bridge for the Metropolitan Railway Company at Christ Church Avenue, new roof for Gibraltar Garrison, Vauxhall Temporary Bridge, 20ft rolling bridge at Fort Borstal, Chatham, gangway bridge of 58ft span for the Netherland Steam Boat Company.

1899 – 350ft span for Kotri Rohri Bridge, four 75ft and ten 550ft spans for the Grand Junction Railway, six spans for the Burma Railway, Poplar Dock Swing and Drawbridge, sluice gates for the Jamrao Canal, Indian Public Works Department, bridge work for the Imperial Chinese Railways.

1900 – Girder work for the Tarkwa Railway, Gold Coast, Africa, spans of various sizes for the Norwegian Trunk Railways, 30ft spans for the East Indian Railway, steel freezing cells for the Atlas Company of Copenhagen, Denmark, spans of various sizes for the Burma Railways, spans of various sizes for the Bengal-Nagpur Railway, steel framework for Mr Beadle's workshop, Dartford, steel roof principals for Messrs Allen's new works at Harrow, cement stock boxes for Bazley, White & Brothers, Swanscombe, superstructure for a small bridge at Wisley, Brentford bridge for the London United Tramways Company, Llanelly Dock Gates, Cliffe Fort Pier for the War Office.

1902 – Caissons for Keyham and Gibraltar, three sets of dock gates for the Tredegar Dry Dock at Newport, steelwork for Folkestone Harbour and a caisson for the Alexandra Dry Dock.

1903 – Twelve floating caissons completed, order for a floating caisson for New Dock, Hong Kong.

1904 – Steel structural work for the Portland Bill Lighthouse.

1905 – 14 metre span bridge for the Buenos Ayres and Pacific Railway Company. Jetty (390ft) for Farmagusta Harbour, Cyprus, six large steel tanks for the Linoleum Manufacturing Company, Staines.

1906 – Three pairs of dock gates for the Swansea Harbour Trust; deck spans for bridges for the Jaipur-Sewai-Madhopur Railway; two bridge spans for the Bombay, Baroda and Central Indian Railway Company. Miike Dock Gates, Japan; iron and steel piles amounting to 210 tons for bridges over the great Brak River, Cape Government Railways; 198ft long steel footbridge for Central South African Railways; six steel water tanks for the Mexican Railway Company; iron and steel bridge carrying the railway near Arundel Junction, London, Brighton and South Coast Railway Company; steel work for the Florentine Court of the Dublin Exhibition; steel trough for the smelting works of Johnson and Sons at Paul Street, Finsbury; landing stage for the Trinity Lighthouse at Cape Pembroke, Falkland Islands.

1907 – Iron jetty for Accra, lighthouse for the new Admiralty Pier at Dover. Various bridges and structural steelwork for India.

1910 – Iron jetty for Lagos Harbour, bridges for South African railways, iron and steelwork for the Tanjong Pagar Wharf, pontoon for a 150 ton floating crane and work in progress included two large floating caissons for the new graving dock at Singapore, and bridge work for India, ten 50ft bridge spans for South Africa, overhead bridge for Bloemfontein, footbridge for East Rand Station, South African Railways.

1911 – Floating caissons for Keppel Harbour Graving Dock, Singapore, contract for the supply of decks for 367 small bridges, Indian State Railways, 6ft spans bridge decks for Ceylon Railways, pair of gates for a dry dock for torpedo boat destroyers, HM Dockyard, Devonport.

(D) Motor vehicles

By 1910 the Thames Iron Works was building a range of motor buses, lorries and cars at their Greenwich Works. In adverts for that year they offered the following range of cars, the Cynosure, the Chirurgeon, the Conqueror, a 12hp touring car and a 15hp touring car. In adverts for that year they proudly proclaimed that the 'Thames' cars hold all worlds records from 50 to 300 miles.

1904 – 1906 Five motor coaches for the London and South Coast Motor Service.

1905 – A four ton steam lorry and 20-30 cwt petrol van exhibited at the Motor Show at the Agricultural Show, Islington.

1906 – Fifteen chassis for the Alliance Motor Company

1910 – On November 5th 1910, new and highly satisfactory records were established on the Brooklands track by the Thames 60hp car, six cylinder engine, 5ins bore, 7ins stroke.

1911 – The London & South Coast Motor Services Ltd – Eight motor char-a-bancs to carry 27 passengers, four cylinder 40hp engines.

1911 – HM Post Office, London, order for 26 motor mail vans.

1911 – New 60hp engine for the 'Thames' racing car.

Abbreviations used in the products list

bm – builder's measurement,	oa – overall
d – displacement	pp – between perpendiculars
hp – horse power	wl – waterline
ihp – indicated horse power	? – unknown value

LIST OF LIFEBOATS BUILT BY THE THAMES IRON WORKS
SHIPBUILDING & ENGINEERING CO. LTD, 1896-1912

Rhyl (34ft 0ins by 8ft 9ins)
Port St. Mary (35ft by 8ft 6ins)
Michael Henry, Newhaven (37ft 0ins by 9ft 3ins)
Sutton (35ft 0ins by 8ft 6ins)
Minnie Moon, Cadgwith (39ft 0ins by 9ft 6ins)
Jane Anni, Irvine (37ft 0ins by 9ft 3ins)
Table Bay (40ft 0ins by 10ft 6ins)
Wicklow (40ft 0ins by 10ft 6ins)
Howth (45ft 0ins by 12ft 6ins)
Southend (38ft 0ins by 12ft 0ins)
George and Jane Walker, Bridlington Quay (35ft 0ins by 8ft 3ins)
James Stevens No 14, Walton-on-Naze (43ft by 12ft 6ins)
Covent Garden, Caister No 1 (40ft 0ins by 12ft 0ins)
Henry Dundas, St. Mary's Scilly (38ft by 9ft 4ins)
James Stevens No 10, St Ives (37ft 6ins by 9ft 3ins)
James Stevens No 12, Swansea (35ft by 8ft 6ins)
Civil Service No 3, Port Patrick (37ft 6ins by 9ft 3ins)
James Stevens No 11, New Romney (35ft 0ins by 8ft 6ins)
James Stevens No 13, Arbroath (35ft 0ins by 8ft 3ins)
Licensed Victualler, Hunstanton (35ft 0ins by 8ft 3ins)
Isabella, Methil & Buckhaven (35ft 0ins by 10ft 0ins)
James Stevens No 15, Wexford (40ft 0ins by 10ft 0ins),
William Arthur Millward, Dunbar (35ft 0ins by 10ft 0ins)
John Francis White, Porthleven (35ft 0ins by 8ft 6ins)
James Stevens No 16, Dungarvan Bay (40ft 0ins by 11ft 0ins)
John Anthony, Cambois (34ft 0ins by 8ft 0ins)
Marianne Atherstone, Montrose No 2 (34ft 0ins by 8ft 0ins)
Sarah Ann Holden, Johnshaven, (35ft 0ins by 8ft 6ins)
George Woodfindin, Sunderland North Dock (37ft 0ins by 9ft 3ins)
James Stevens No 17, Porthoustock (36ft 0ins by 9ft 0ins)
James Stevens No 18, Girvan (35ft 0ins by 10ft 0ins)
John William Dudley, Winchelsea (35ft 0ins by 8ft 6ins)
Joseph Whitworth, Holy Island No 2 (34ft 0ins x 8ft 0ins)
Forester, Tynemouth No 2 (34ft 0ins by 8ft 0ins)
John Wesley, Barry Dock (43ft by 12ft 6ins)
James Stevens No 20, Queenstown (43ft 0ins by 12ft 6ins)
Constance Melanie, Coverack (35ft 0ins by 10ft 0ins)
James Stevens No 19, Newburgh (34ft 0ins by 8ft 0ins)
John Groome, Killough (35ft 0ins by 10ft 0ins)
Chapman, Groomsport (35ft 0ins by 10ft 0ins)
Thomas Fielden, Piel, Barrow, (40ft 0ins by 11ft 0ins)
Albert Edward, Clackton-on-Sea (45ft 0ins by 12ft 6ins)

City of Winchester, *a non-righting lifeboat of the Norfolk and Suffolk type built by the Thames Iron Works for Aldeburgh.*

Mary Hamer Hoyle, Dover (37ft 6ins by 9ft 3ins)
Sarah Jane Turner, Montrose No 1 (37ft 0ins by 9ft 3ins)
Worthing (35ft 0ins by 8ft 6ins)
Vezia Gwilt, Courtmacsherry (37ft 6ins by 9ft 3ins)
Ida, Huna (37ft 0ins by 9ft 3ins)
54th West Norfolk Regiment, Palling No 1(37ft 6ins by 9ft 3ins)
Charles Arcoll, Hastings (35ft 0ins by 8ft 6ins)
Sarah Pilkington, Stornoway (35ft 0ins by 8ft 6ins)
Matthew Middlewood, Flamborough No 2 (35ft 0ins by 8ft 3ins)
Ed Harvey, Padstow No 2 (42ft by 11ft 6ins)
George and Margaret, Whithorn (35ft 0ins by 8ft 6ins)
George Leicester, Minehead (35ft 0ins by 10ft 0ins)
George and Mary Berrey, Banff (35ft by 8ft 6ins)
Barbara Fleming, Porthdinllaen (40ft 0ins by 10ft 6ins)
City of Winchester, Aldeburgh (46ft 0ins by 14ft 0ins)
Mary Andrew, Hauxley (34ft 0ins by 8ft 0ins)
Queensbury, Scarborough (35ft 0ins by 8ft 3ins)
Robert and Catherine, Appledore No 2 (34ft 0ins by 8ft 0ins)

Sarah Kay. Built for the Dunbar (Skateraw) station which was opened in 1907.

Theodore Price, Llandudno (37ft 0ins by 9ft 3ins)
Wighton, Torquay (38ft 0ins by 9ft 4ins)
Colonel Stock, Western-Super-Mare (38ft 0ins by 9ft 4ins)
Ryder, Looe (35ft 0ins by 8ft 6ins)
La Totitam, Aranmore (37ft 0ins x 9ft 3ins)
Rose Beddington, Drogheda (35ft 0ins by 8ft 3ins)
Brittan Willis, Freencastle (35ft 0ins by 8ft 6ins)
William Maynard, Skerries (35ft 0ins by 10ft 0ins)
Hopwood, Portrush (35ft 0ins by 10ft 0ins)
Louisa Hartwell, Cromer (38ft 0ins by 10ft 9ins)
The Sisters, Kilmore (35ft 0ins by 8ft 6ins)
William and Mary Devey, Tenby (38ft 0ins by 9ft 4ins)
Philip Beach, Burnham (35ft 0ins by 10ft 0ins)
Mary Ann Lockwood, Robin Hood's Bay (34ft 0ins x 8ft 6ins)
William and Charles, Whitburn (35ft 0ins by 8ft 3ins)
Dash, Blyth (35ft 0ins by 8ft 6ins)
Norman Clarke, North Berwick (35ft 0ins by 8ft 6ins)
Robert Fleming, Totland Bay (37ft 0ins x 9ft 3ins)

John and Amy, Hendon Beach (34ft 0ins by 8ft 10ins)
William Roberts, Littlehaven (40ft 0ins by 11ft 0ins)
Nancy Lucy, Caister No 2 (35ft 0ins by 10ft 9ins)
Elizabeth Leicester, Whitehaven (35ft 0ins by 8ft 6ins)
Leslie, Folkestone (35ft 0ins by 8ft 6ins)
Admiral Sir George Back, The Lizard (35ft 0ins by 8ft 6ins)
John Lingard Ross, Watchet (35ft 0ins by 8ft 9ins)
Olive, Eastbourne No 2 (36ft 0ins by 9ft 0ins)
Matthew Simpson, Berwick-on-Tweed (37ft 0ins by 9ft 3ins)
Friern Watch, Weymouth (38ft 0ins by 9ft 4ins)
Alexandra, Hope Cove (35ft 0ins by 10ft 0ins)
James William and Caroline Courtney, Fowey (35ft 0ins by 9ft 0ins)
Charles Deere James, St Agnes, Scilly (38ft 0ins by 10ft 0ins)
Ann Fawcett, Harwich No1 (43ft 0ins by 12ft 6ins)
John Harling, Southport (43ft 6ins by 13ft 3ins)
Joseph Somes, Exmouth (35ft 0ins by 8ft 6ins)
Horatio Brand, Hartlepool No 3 (35ft 0ins by 8ft 6ins)
James and Mary Walker, Anstruther (38ft 0ins by 9ft 4ins)

Minehead lifeboat being launched. George Leicester commenced service at the station in 1901 and is credited with saving 23 lives before retirement in 1927.

Arriving at the Filey station in 1907 Hollon the Third *was 35ft by 8ft 3ins and fitted with two ballast tanks and a drop keel.*

Richard, Donna Nook (34ft 0ins by 8ft 0ins)
John Fortune, Port Erroll (38ft 0ins by 9ft 4ins)
William and Emma, Salcombe (35ft 0ins by 10ft 0ins)
Burbie, Troon (38ft 0ins by 9ft 4ins)
Charles Burton, Grimsby (38ft 0ins by 10ft 9ins)
Michael Smart, Yealm River (35ft 0ins by 8ft 6ins)
James Cullen, Bull Bay (38ft 0ins by 9ft 4ins)
John R Ker, Southend, Cantyre (38ft 0ins by 9ft 4ins)
Oldham, Abersoch (38ft 0ins by 9ft 4ins)
Brothers Freeman, Littlehampton (35ft 0ins by 8ft 6ins)
William Restell, Shoreham (35ft 0ins by 8ft 6ins)
Thomas Lingham, Rhosneigr (34ft 0ins by 8ft 0ins)
William Brocksopp, Aberdovey (35ft by 8ft 6ins)
Charlie Medland, The Mumbles (43ft 0ins by 12ft 6ins)
J C Madge, Sheringham (41ft 0ins by 11ft 0ins)
Charles & Susanna Stephens, Ramsgate (43ft 0ins by 12ft 0ins)
Jones-Gibb, Barmouth (38ft 0ins by 9ft 4ins)
William Wallis, Brighton (35ft 0ins by 8ft 6ins)
Ellen & Margaret of Settle, Hornsea (34ft 0ins by 8ft 6ins)
James Finlayson, Lossiemouth (35ft 0ins by 9ft 0ins)

John Rowson Lingard, Mablethorpe (36ft 0ins by 9ft 0ins)

Kentwell, Lowestoft (46ft 0ins by 12ft 6ins)

Civil Service No 5, Maryport (38ft 0ins by 9ft 4ins)

Edward Z Dresden, Aldeburgh No 2, (38ft 0ins by 10ft 9ins)

Helen Blake, Fethard (35ft 0ins by 8ft 6ins)

Elizabeth Austin, Cardigan (35ft 0ins by 8ft 6ins)

William & Harriot, Ballantrae (35ft 0ins by 8ft 10ins)

Forester, Flamboro No 1 (35ft 0ins by 8ft 3ins)

Ann Miles, Longhope (43ft 0ins by 12ft 6ins)

Selina, Ryde (30ft 0ins by 7ft 3ins)

Charles Dibdin, North Deal (43ft 0ins by 12ft 0ins)

John, Cloughey (35ft 0ins by 10ft 0ins)

Samuel Lewis, Skegness (35ft 0ins by 10ft 0ins)

Hannah Fawsett Bennett, Hoylake (38ft 0ins by 10ft 0ins)

Marianne, Newcastle (35ft 0ins by 8ft 6ins)

Forster Fawsett, North Sunderland (35ft 0ins by 8ft 3ins)

Prichard Frederick Gainer, Lynmouth (35ft 0ins by 8ft 6ins)

Janet, Port Eynon (35ft 0ins by 8ft 6ins)

Maria, Broughty Ferry (40ft 0ins by 11ft 0ins, motor boat)

John A Hay, Stromness (42ft 0ins by 11ft 6ins, motor boat)

John and Naomi Beattie, Aberystwyth (35ft 0ins by 8ft 6ins)

Charterhouse, Fishguard (40ft 0ins by 10ft 6ins, motor boat)

Marianne L Hay, Youghal (35ft 0ins by 8ft 6ins)

John Ryburn, Stronsay (43ft 0ins by 12ft 6ins, motor boat)

Ada Lewis, Newbiggin (37ft 0ins by 8ft 6ins)

Admiral Rodd, Hayle (36ft 0ins by 8ft 3ins)

The Gem, Atherfield (35ft 0ins by 8ft 6ins)

Sarah Kay, Skateraw, Dunbar (35ft 0ins by 10ft 0ins)

Hollon the Third, Filey, (35ft 0ins by 8ft 3ins)

Co-operator No 1, Cullercoats (37ft 0ins by 8ft 6ins)

James Gowland, Staithes, (35ft 0ins by 8ft 3ins)

Elinor Roget, Clovelly (37ft 6ins by 9ft 3ins)

Brothers Brickwood, Brightstone Grange (35ft 0ins by 8ft 6ins)

Thomas McCunn, Port Logan (35ft 0ins by 8ft 10ins)

Francis Whitburn, Seaton Carew (35ft 0ins by 8ft 3ins)

Fifi and Charles, Redcar (35ft 0ins by 8ft 3ins)

William Cantwell Ashby, Newquay (35ft 0ins by 10ft 0ins)

Susan Ashley, Brooke (35ft 0ins by 8ft 6ins)

Hasborough (34ft 0ins by 8ft 0ins)

Maria Stephenson, Buckie (38ft 0ins by 9ft 4ins)

Co-operator No 3, Ackergill (37ft 0ins by 9ft 3ins)

Charles Henry Ashley, Cemaes (38ft 0ins by 9ft 4ins)

Richard Ashley, Ferryside (37ft 6ins by 9ft 3ins)

Sarah Austin, Thurso (40ft 0ins by 11ft 0ins)

Caroline, Blakeney (38ft 0ins by 10ft 9ins)

James Scarlett, St. Anne's (36ft 0ins by 9ft 0ins)

Robert and Mary Ellis, Whitby No 1 (35ft 0ins by 8ft 6ins)
Eleanor Brown, Winterton No 2 (44ft 6ins by 12ft 6ins)
Charles Deere James, St Agnes (38ft 0ins by 9ft 4ins)
Helmsdale (28ft 0ins by 7ft 0ins)
John and Robert C Mercer, Alnmouth (34ft 0ins by 8ft 0ins)
Anne Frances, Eyemouth (35ft 0ins by 8ft 6ins)
General R Dudley Blake, Black Rock (35ft 0ins by 8ft 3ins)
William Riley, Upgang (34ft 0ins by 8ft 0ins)
William and Laura, Donagadee (43ft 0ins by 12ft 6ins)
Richard Crawley, Southsea (37ft 0ins by 9ft 3ins)
Lizzie Porter, Holy Island (35ft 0ins by 8ft 6ins)
Brother and Sister, Llanddulas (36ft 0ins by 9ft 0ins)
Martha, Cresswell (34ft 0ins by 8ft 0ins)
John and Sarah Hatfield, St Andrews (35ft 0ins by 8ft 10ins)
Edwin Kay, Crail (35ft 0ins by 8ft 10ins)
Elliot Galer, Seaham (38ft 0ins by 10ft 0ins, motor boat)
Helen Smitten, St Abbs (38ft 0ins by 10ft 0ins, motor boat)
Janet Hoyle, Ayr (35ft 0ins by 10ft 0ins)
Charles and Eliza Laura, Moelfre (40ft 0ins by 11ft 0ins)
George Gordon Moir, Kirkcudbright (35ft 0ins by 8ft 10ins)
Lisbon (35ft 0ins by 8ft 6ins)
James Leath, Pakefield (42ft 0ins by 12ft 6ins)
Harmar, Poole (37ft 6ins by 9ft 3ins)
Robert Theophilus Garden, Wicklow (40ft 0ins by 10ft 6ins, motor boat)
Mayer de Rothschild, Hythe (35ft 0ins by 8ft 6ins)
Jane Hannah Macdonald, Appledore No 1 (35ft 0ins by 8ft 6ins)
Hester Rothschild, Runswick (35ft 0ins by 8ft 10ins)
Henry Vernon, Tynemouth (40ft 0ins by 10ft 6ins, motor boat)
St. Davids (40ft 0ins by 10ft 6ins, motor boat)
John Watson Wakefield, Poolbeg (30ft 0ins by 7ft 3ins)
Elizabeth Moore Garden, Bude (35ft 0ins by 8ft 10ins)
Fanny Harriet, Dunmore East (37ft 0ins by 9ft 3ins)
Henry Finlay, Machrihanish (35ft 0ins by 8ft 6ins)
Arthur R Dawes, Boulmer (35ft 0ins by 8ft 10ins)
Campletown (43ft 0ins by 12ft 6ins)
Beaumaris (43ft 0ins by 12ft 6ins)
Peterhead (43ft 0ins by 12ft 6ins)
Withernsea (34ft 0ins by 8ft 0ins)
Criccieth (35ft 0ins by 8ft 10ins)
St. Helier (35ft 0ins by 8ft 6ins)
St. Peter Port (35ft 0ins by 10ft 0ins)
Lytham (35ft 0ins by 8ft 6ins)
Newhaven (38ft 0ins by 9ft 9ins)
Yarmouth (34ft 0ins by 10ft 0ins)

Hoylake lifeboat Hannah Fawsett Bennett *pictured with Coxswain Thomas Dodd was in service from 1908 till 1931.*

A 3 ton locomotive steam crane as manufactured by the Thames Iron Works and Shipbuilding Company.

Mircea, *a 390 tons training brig with screw engines built for the Romanian government by the Thames Iron Works in 1882.*

Samoyed *under the shears at the Thames Iron Works in 1895. This ship was a survey and supply vessel for the Russian Navy and was launched in 1894.*

Captain Belaieff with his officers and crew photographed on the after deck of the Samoyed. *The photograph was taken in 1894 at the handing over of the ship to the Russian government.*

Boadicea, *a Thames paddle steamer built by the Thames Iron Works in 1897. Here the vessel is photographed on the Thames at Lambeth Palace.*

Thames, *a River Thames Conservancy paddle yacht built by the Thames Iron Works in 1881.*

A Thames Iron Works lifeboat built for the National Lifeboat Institution in 1896.

LEFT: *The valve gear of the Walton triple expansion steam engines under construction in the workshops of the Thames Iron Works, 1911.*

RIGHT: *One of the triple expansion steam engines constructed for the Walton pumping station, 1911.*

One of the steam engines constructed by the Thames Iron Works for the 56ft steam pinnaces for the Admiralty.

Dock gates constructed by the Thames Iron Works for the Tredegar Dry Dock Company, Newport, 1901.

LEFT: *A 150ft span for the Shalimar Ferry, Bengal, Nagpur Railway photographed at the Thames Iron Works in 1901.*

RIGHT: *Thames Iron Works gates for the Torpedo Boat Destroyer Dock, HM Dockyard, Devonport, 1911.*

The Barking Road Bridge constructed by the Thames Iron Works in 1896.

The Ilford footbridge built by the Thames Iron Works in 1896.

One of three 300 tons coaling lighters fitted with Temperley Transporters built by the Thames Iron Works for the Admiralty, 1903.

A 40hp motor coach built by the Thames Iron Works in 1906 for the London & South Coast Motor Service.

The Hone's patent Grab was an important engineering product for the Thames Iron Works in the company's later history. Here is an example photographed in the works' yard in 1895.

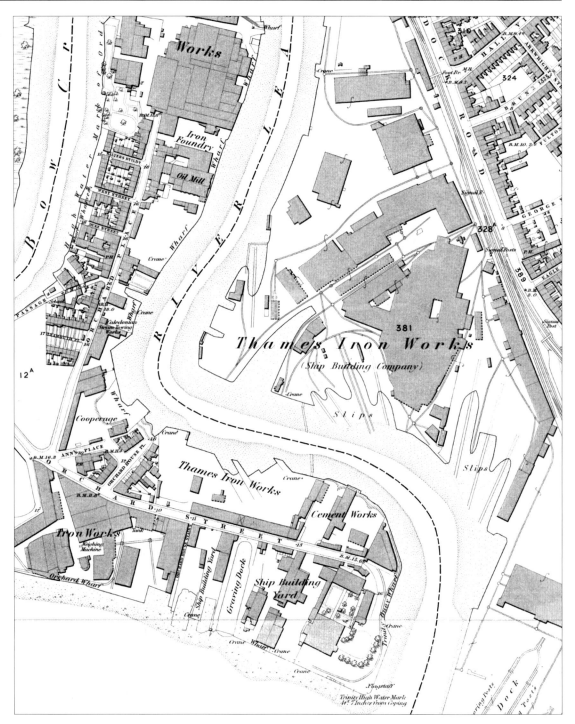

Thames Iron Works site from 25 inch Ordnance Survey map first edition 1869.

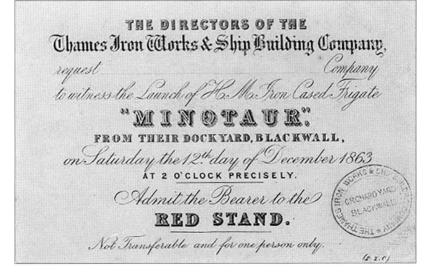

ABOVE: Tavarez-Trigueiros, *a twin screw tug built for the State Railways of Portugal. The ship was launched by the Thames Iron Works in 1902.*

LEFT: *An invitation card to the Launch of HMS* Minotaur *in 1863.*
- ERIC PEMBERTON
isleofdogslife.wordpress.com

Bibliography & Sources

1. Laurence Ince, *The Soho Engine Works, 1796 – 1895*, Stationary Power, The Journal of the International Stationary Steam Engine Society, No 16, 2000, p. 33.

2. Laurence Ince, Maudslay,Sons & Field, 1831 – 1904, in *Henry Maudslay & The Pioneers Of The Machine Age* (Stroud 2002), p. 168.

3. J. Grantham, *Iron as a Material for Ship-Building* (1842) p. 5.

4. Memoir of the Late T. J. Ditchburn, *Transactions of the Royal Institution of Naval Architects*, Volume 11, 1870, pp. 233 – 246.

5. *Thames Iron Works Gazette, (TIWG)* June 1898, pp. 116 – 118.

6. A. J. Arnold, *Iron Shipbuilding on the Thames, 1832 – 1915* (Aldershot 2000) , pp. 28 – 29.

7. Baring Archives, HC 1, 106 – 2, Steam boats, 1843, Ditchburn & Mare Documents.

8. *The Times*, 8 May 1848.

9. *The Sydney Morning Herald*, 19 August 1847.

10. *TIWG*, June 1898, p. 118.

11. *TIWG*, Volume 2, 1896, p. 3.

12. Philip Banbury, *Shipbuilders of the Thames and Medway* (Newton Abbot 1971), p. 233.

13. A. J. Arnold, *Iron Shipbuilding on the Thames, 1832 – 1915* (Aldershot 2000), p. 61.

14. *The Times*, 26 January 1857, p. 7.

15. A. J. Arnold, *Iron Shipbuilding on the Thames, 1832-1915* (Aldershot 2000), p. 62.

16. *The Times*, 3 September 1860, p. 10.

17. A. J. Arnold, *Iron Shipbuilding on the Thames, 1832-1915* (Aldershot 2000), p. 92.

18. P. Barry, *Dockyard Economy and Naval Power* (1863), pp. 209-220.

19. A. J. Arnold, *Iron Shipbuilding on the Thames*, 1832 – 1915 (Aldershot 2000), p. 94.

20. F. C. Bowen, Shipbuilders of other days: The Thames Ironworks, *Shipbuilding and Shipping Record*, Vol 22 (1945) pp. 375-6.

21. *The Times*, 18 January 1867, p. 10.

22. *TIWG*, Volume 3, 1897, p. 58.

23. *TIWG* Volume 7, 1902, p. 114.

24. *TIWG*, Volume 8, 1903, pp. 6-10.

25. A. J. Arnold, *Iron Shipbuilding on the Thames, 1832 – 1915* (Aldershot 2000), p. 112.

26. A. J. Arnold, *Iron Shipbuilding on the Thames, 1832 -1915* (Aldershot 2000), p. 137.

27. London Metropolitan Archives (LMA), Minute book and annual reports and accounts for the Thames Iron Works, Shipbuilding and Engineering Company limited 1899 – 1911 (TIWMINB), first general meeting, 30 October 1899.

28. LMA, TIWMINB, O/45/1, first annual report for the year ending December 1899.

29. LMA, TIWMINB, O/45/1, second annual general meeting, Wednesday April 3 1901, second annual report for the year ending December 1900.

30. LMA, TIWMINB, O/45/1,third annual general meeting, 9 April 1902.

31. LMA, TIWMINB, O/45/1, fourth annual general meeting, 8 April 1903.

32. *Proceedings of the Institution of Mechanical Engineers*, 1900, pp. 494-496.

33. LMA, TIWMINB, O/45/1, fifth annual general meeting, 11 April 1904.

34. LMA, TIWMINB, O/45/1, sixth annual general meeting, 12 April 1905.

35. LMA, TIWMINB, O/45/1, seventh annual general meeting, 11 April 1906.

36. LMA, TIWMINB, O/45/1, eighth annual general meeting,, 11 April 1907.

37. LMA, TIWMINB, O/45/1, ninth annual general meeting, 9 April 1908.

38. LMA, TIWMINB, O/45/1, tenth annual general meeting, 14 May 1909.

39. LMA, TIWMINB, O/45/1, eleventh annual general meeting, April 1910.

40. Laurence Ince, *Neath Abbey and the Industrial Revolution* (Stroud 2001), p.44.

41. *The Engineer*, December 13, 1895. This issue has been printed with the wrong date as December 13 1894.

42. Captain John Wells RN, *The Immortal Warrior, Britain's First and Last Battleship* (Emsworth 1987), pp. 37-38.

43. David Lyon, *The First Destroyers* (1996), pp. 90-91.

44. *The Tablet*, 29 August 1959, p. 12.

45. David Howarth and Stephen Howarth, *The Story of P&O* (1986), pp. 10-12.

46. Laurence Ince, *The South Wales Iron Industry, 1750 – 1885* (Solihull 1993), p.148. The Millwall Company showed more than a passing interest when the Brynna Ironworks was put for sale in 1862.

47. James Laming, *What is to be done with the General Screw Steam Shipping Company's fleet of ships when no longer needed for the Government Service – answered by showing that the trade with India may be re-opened with advantage* (1855).

Note : The ship list on page 115 has been constructed from several sources, the main ones are, *Thames Historical Catalogue* (1911), and A. J. Arnold, *Iron Shipbuilding on the Thames 1832 -1915* (Aldershot 2000), pp. 156-186. However, these are only basic lists and the Ditchburn & Mare list lacks many important ships built by the partnership. I have added much information regarding the ships and given some of the histories of these vessels. The main sources have been, *Conways All the World's Fighting Ships 1860-1905*, (1979), *Henry Maudslay, 171-1831: and Maudslay, Sons & Field, Ltd (1949)*, Laurence Ince, *The Soho Engine Works 1796-1895*, Stationary Power, the Journal of the International Stationary Steam Engine Society, No 16, 2000, Robert Murray, *Rudimentary Treatise on the Marine Engine and on Steam Vessels and the Screw* (1858), Frank L Dix, *Royal River Highway* (Newton Abbot, 1985), Richard Hartree, *John Penn and Sons of Greenwich* (2008), particularly the author's list of ships engined by the firm and Frank Burtt, *Steamers of the Thames and Medway* (1949). Particularly useful has been the historical information gleaned from P&O's excellent heritage websites which contains histories of all the company's ships (www.poheritage.com).

Index